TRADING

DEBT

FOR

WEALTH

The ideas in this book have helped many people to dramatically improve their financial situation and enjoy a happier, lower-stress lifestyle. Your results may vary. The author does not accept responsibility for the results of any actions taken by readers. THIS BOOK IS NOT LEGAL ADVICE or financial advice for any specific person's unique situation. If you have a legal question, please consult an attorney. If you need financial advice specific to your situation, please consult the appropriate financial professional.

DEDICATION

For my smart, sweet, beautiful daughter, Kristi. You are
a wonderful person, and your daddy is proud of you.

TABLE OF CONTENTS

(STEP FIVE – continued):

INTRODUCTION

Congratulations! You've just made a great investment. This workbook is designed to help you do exactly what the title indicates – get out from under all your debt, much more quickly than you probably believe to be possible, and to start on a program of rapidly accumulating wealth for your retirement.

If you're like many people, you probably have so much debt that you can't afford to save for your future. You may have no idea how you're going to retire, let alone how you will be able to do all the things you once planned on doing when you do retire.

There is no magic in this workbook – it's just math. But learning the concepts taught in this workbook can produce results that might seem magical. And these concepts are easy to learn, simple to implement, and very effective if used consistently.

No one can give you a magic dollar that comes back to you every time you spend it. But the dollar you now have might be worth over ten dollars to you, once you learn the concepts taught in this workbook.

These techniques have been tested and proven. Although these concepts are not as widely known as they should be, they have been used successfully by many people, who have become financially independent as a result. After studying this book, you will be able to exercise better financial judgment; and that can make your life a lot more pleasant than it may have been before.

Here's another good thing about the concepts in this workbook. You don't have to be skilled, talented, or lucky to benefit from them. All you have to do is use them. And virtually anybody can, if they learn how. This workbook will take you through the learning process, step by step.

This workbook was written for the non-financial professional, intended to be easy to understand and to use. So don't worry about complex financial concepts and formulas, just enjoy a simple learning process that will change the way you think about and use your money forever. And use the spaces provided to take notes. If you will learn to utilize the simple concepts that follow, they could add $1,000,000 or more to your retirement fund.

[Note: This book has been recently updated, and interest rates have changed since this was originally written. Though the numbers may change over time, the concepts remain the same and consistently produce positive results.]

STEP #1

UNDERSTANDING COMPOUND INTEREST

The first thing you must do if you want to trade in your debt for wealth is to understand how compound interest works. When you truly understand how compound interest can affect you and your long-term financial status, then you will be able to develop productive attitudes and habits regarding the paying and receiving of compound interest.

A wealthy man I worked for as a teenager once told me, "[Rico], there are two kinds of people in this world – those who understand compound interest and *collect* it, and those who don't – and *pay* it."

There is a horrible disease that has infected the United States in recent years; and it seems to be spreading worldwide. You can call it impatience, the need for instant gratification, or whatever you like. But the problem is this: people don't save up and pay cash for things anymore!

It used to be that if you wanted to buy something nice for yourself, your spouse or your children, you saved your money then bought it when you could afford it.

That or you put it on layaway and took it home after you paid it off. Here's an important fact that hardly anyone seems to realize anymore:

If you can't pay cash for it, you can't afford it!

Let's think about this for a minute. What does it mean to be able to *afford* something? It means that you can pay for it – with your own money – without jeopardizing anything else that's important, right? If you can't even pay for it with your own money, can you really afford it?

When buying something on credit, most people think in terms of being able to afford the payments, not the item. They look at what the "low, low monthly payment" will be and imagine that they can fit that into their budget somehow – and that means they can afford the item in question.

But thinking that you can afford the payments is very different from actually being able to afford to purchase the item itself. The fact that you have to borrow the money to purchase something means that you cannot afford it!

Now, I'm not going to tell you that you can't have any fun anymore. And I'm not going to tell you that all debt is evil. The fact is, debt can be good or bad, depending on how you use it.

What I want to accomplish in this section, is simply to help you see how your debt will affect you and your family in the long run. When you start using compound interest instead of letting it use you, you'll wind up having a lot more fun – and being able to buy more of the things that help make life fun. And you'll be able to afford them.

Let's look at a theoretical example to illustrate how debt can affect your financial status.

Let's say that you and your spouse want to take a well-deserved vacation. You can save up for it, or you can put it on a brand new credit card you just got in the mail. If you put it on a credit card, you can go *now*. That sounds great, doesn't it? I know; I've done it.

Let's say this vacation costs $3,000 – not an expensive vacation. You can put aside $250 per month in a savings account, and go in a year; or you can charge it, leave now, and make a much smaller minimum monthly payment on your credit card when you return.

It's not too difficult to figure out which one of these options is going to be more popular nowadays, especially if $250 a month doesn't fit into the budget. But, let's look at the long-term effects of this decision.

Let's say you charged the $3,000 on your new credit card and went on vacation. When you get back, you receive the bill and you make the minimum monthly payment, on time, every month. Let's assume, for purposes of this example, that the minimum monthly payment is 3% of the total outstanding balance, including interest accrued, and that the interest rate charged by the credit card is 19.95%.

Your first payment is only $91.50. Not bad compared to the $250 per month you would have had to put aside every month for a whole year, just to take the trip a year later if you paid cash, right?

Let's also assume that you put new charges on your credit card of just under $50 every month. This is the amount of credit you would have available after you make your minimum payment every month, if your credit limit were $3,000, the amount of your vacation. This is a very realistic scenario. Most people's credit situation is far worse than this. This is only one credit card that stays charged to the limit – many people have several, and some with substantially higher credit limits than this.

Let's say that you were 30 years old when you took this trip, and that you kept your credit card charged to its limit with that small, under $50 monthly charge, until age 65, when you received some retirement funds and paid your balance in full.

The approximately $50 you charged on your credit card every month is the same amount that your monthly payment reduced your principal balance. (Your $91.50 payment is approximately $50 principal and $41.50 interest.) We could say that, effectively, you were paying cash for all these purchases, right? (The $50 you charge every month is being paid back by your $50 principal payment.)

That would leave your vacation responsible for the interest paid all these years, right? (I'm trying to simulate the effect of paying only interest and deferring the principal repayment of the initial $3,000 charge, because this is how many people use their credit cards. Read the last two paragraphs again if you need to.)

Let's see how much this vacation really cost you, since you charged it on your credit card instead of paying cash. $91.50 per month multiplied by 35 years (420 months), minus the $50 per month in new charges, equals $17,430. Add that to the $3,000 you paid from your retirement fund to close out the debt, and the grand total for your vacation is $20,430. That's a lot more than the $3,000 you intended to pay, isn't it?

But this is only part of the picture. Let's say that instead of going on vacation, you had decided to put the $41.50 you spent on interest for 35 years ($91.50 payment less $50 in new purchases) into an IRA with a yield of 12% per year. When you turn 65, you have $266,885 in your account (plus the $3,000 you didn't have to use to pay off your credit card). Your vacation cost you a whopping $269,885!

I'm not suggesting that you should never go on vacation. I'm not suggesting that you should never buy anything nice for your family or yourself. I am suggesting that you need to realize the effects of paying compound interest versus receiving compound interest. Before borrowing money for something, you should think about these three questions:

(1) How much will this have cost me after I've made all the payments?

(2) How much could I accumulate if I were to make the same payment into a retirement account, instead of going into debt?

(3) How much more could I get for the same amount of money this will cost me if I were to save up and pay cash?

Let's return to the above example for a moment. This is probably not your exact situation, but it illustrates the effects of receiving instead of paying compound interest (or returns on investment, in general).

You may be thinking, "No one is really going to keep charging up their credit card so they have to pay on it for 35 years." Well, guess what? Even if you hadn't made one additional charge on the card, but made only the minimum monthly payment; on average, it would take approximately 40 years to get it paid off! That's even longer than in the example.

And we all know that when people are strapped for cash because their bills are too high, they generally only make the minimum payment, and hope that they can pay more next time (and they rarely do).

I said earlier that debt can be good or bad, depending on how you use it. Let me now clarify that statement. Debt is bad for you much more frequently than it is good for you. When can debt be good for you? Here are a few examples:

(1) When it allows you to buy a home instead of renting one on a long-term basis;

(2) When it allows you to obtain the education you need to earn a comfortable living;

(3) When it allows you to drive a reliable automobile that you otherwise could not;

(4) When it can provide you or a loved-one with necessary medical care;

(5) When it allows you to pursue a profitable business opportunity;

(6) When it allows you to increase your investment returns. (This may or may not be a good idea, and is beyond the scope of this workbook.)

There are more examples that could be listed here of situations where going into debt could possibly be a wise decision. But, the main point I want to make is this:

Consumer debt should be avoided whenever possible.

Consumer debt is debt used to pay for consumer goods and services. If everyone were to pay cash for all of their consumer goods and services (saving up for things, if necessary), then put what they saved in finance charges into a retirement account, most people would be able to retire comfortably – instead of the only 5% who actually do.

Another important point, while we're on the subject, is this:

> **Just because it may have been wise to *go* into debt for a particular purpose, does not mean that it is wise to *stay* in debt any longer than necessary.**

Here's an obvious example. Let's assume that you are a 100-pound, single woman who has to drive through a high-crime area of town at 11:30 PM every night on your way home from work. It may be better to drive a reliable car than one that breaks down, even if that means going into debt. But, should you really take five or six years to pay that car off?

The same thing goes for a house. It is a rare person that can actually pay cash for a house. But, it can still be a good idea to buy one, even if it means going into debt. However, what if you could pay off your house in half the time or less? What would that mean to your long-term financial situation?

Having to borrow money to purchase a car should be a temporary situation. If you learn and use the concepts taught in this book, within a very reasonable period of time you should be able to pay cash for your cars and vacations, and own your home outright. Then you will know how good it feels to be financially independent.

_____

What things could you have waited to purchase in order to avoid debt and have a more prosperous future?

_____

How Compound Interest Works

So far we've gone over an example to illustrate the effects of compound interest in a common situation. But I really want to make sure that you understand how it works. The system taught in this workbook is extremely effective, but I believe that a person first has to understand how compound interest works because if you don't really understand it, I don't think you can have the necessary judgment or motivation to stick with a program that requires the self-discipline to change your behavior.

Once you get a grasp on how this concept of compound interest really works, and you can see how using it to your advantage instead of letting it be used against you can really change your life, then you have a reason to stick with the program even when you're faced with the temptation to make impulsive decisions that will not benefit you in the long run.

Okay – brace yourself. Don't be scared. We're going to do some math. I know that some of you reading this are probably not too fond of math – and a few of you may even be downright math-hostile. That's okay. Even if you don't want to work the numbers yourself, you will still get a feel for how this works – and that's what we're really after here. You don't have to become a financial planner, but you do need to get a feel for the long-term effects of compound interest or you won't have the ability to make the wisest financial decisions possible when choices come up.

So let's read through the math that follows and those of you who like numbers, please feel free to grab your calculators and work the problems as we go along.

The easiest way to explain how *Compound Interest* works is to first explain how *Simple Interest* works, then show you the difference. Simple interest has a simple formula:

$$I = P \times R \times T$$

In English, that means that the amount of interest you will pay on a simple interest loan is equal to the amount of principal you borrowed multiplied by the annual rate of interest charged, multiplied by the amount of time you borrowed the money for; or…

Interest Charge = Principal × Rate of Interest × Time (number of periods)

When I refer to the number of periods of time, that is in relation to the interest rate percentage charged. For example, normally we think of a given interest rate as the amount of interest charged "per annum", or for one year. If we are paying interest for two years at an annual rate of 12%, we are paying for two "periods" so our interest is actually 24% (plus compounding). We still call the interest rate 12% – but we're paying that 12% twice.

Similarly, if you're paying an interest rate of 12% per year, but the loan is only for six months, you're only paying 6% because you're only paying for half the year.

Let's illustrate the concept of simple interest with an example. Let's say that you borrow $100 from a friend and your friend wants 12% interest to use the money for 1 year. Here's how you use the simple interest formula above to calculate your interest charge:

$$I = P \times R \times T$$

$$I = \$100 \times 12\% \times 1 \text{ year}$$

$$I = \$12$$

Here's what you will have to pay your friend at the end of that year:

$100	Principal Borrowed
+ $12	Interest Charge for One Year ($100 × 12% × 1 year)
$112	Total

Pretty simple, right? Now let's work the same example, only let's say that you borrowed the money for two years:

$$I = P \times R \times T$$

$$I = \$100 \times 12\% \times 2 \text{ years}$$

$$I = \$24$$

Here's what you will have to pay your friend at the end of two years:

$100	Principal Borrowed
+ $24	Interest Charge for Two Years ($100 × 12% × 2 years)
$124	Total

Since we know that 12% interest on $100 equals $12, we can simply multiply the number of years we borrow the $100 by our yearly $12 interest charge. For example, if you borrow the $100 from your friend for 5 years, you will have to pay $60 in interest charges because $12 × 5 years = $60.

That is how simple interest works. Simple, indeed. Compound interest is a little more complicated, but once you understand how it works, it's really not that difficult to work with. And knowing the long-term impact of compound interest is very valuable. Once you understand this, you'll know why it is so important to receive compound interest instead of paying compound interest.

A simple interest loan may require that you pay the interest accrued each year when it comes due. That way, when the next year starts you're still only borrowing the original amount of money – but you're borrowing it for another "term", or in this case, year. Compound interest does not require that you pay the interest accrued at the end of each period.

Compound interest takes the interest you owe at the end of a compounding period (one year in our example) and adds it onto the principal owed at the end of that period. This total becomes the new principal balance at the beginning of the next compounding period. That means that when your interest is compounded for the next period, you're actually paying interest on top of interest.

To make this more clear, let's take the same example we used above only work it using compound interest instead of simple interest. If we say that the annual interest rate is 12% and our compounding period is one year, here's how our example will look the first year:

$$I = P \times R \times T$$

$$I = \$100 \times 12\% \times 1 \text{ year}$$

$$I = \$12$$

Here's the total you owe:

$100	Principal Borrowed
+ $12	Interest Charge for One Year ($100 × 12% × 1 year)
$112	Total

You probably noticed that this is the exact same result as in the simple interest example. Yes, it is. That is because we're only using one compounding period and our period is one year. But look what happens when you borrow the money for two years using compound interest:

Year #1:

$100	Principal Borrowed
+ $12	Interest Charge ($100 × 12% × 1 year)
$112	Balance Owed at End of Year #1

Year #2:

$112.00	Balance from Year #1
× 12%	Interest Rate for Year #2
$13.44	Interest Charge for Year #2

$112.00	Principal for Year #2 (Balance from Year #1, above)
+ $13.44	Interest Charge for Year #2
$125.44	Balance Owed at End of Year #2

Notice that because your second year's interest was charged on $112 instead of on $100, the second year's interest charge is slightly higher. It doesn't look like much of a difference, and it's really not – not yet, anyway. Let's extend the example to five years so we can see how things start to change.

Year #3:

$125.44	Balance from Year #2
× 12%	Interest Rate for Year #3
$15.05	Interest Charge for Year #3
$125.44	Principal for Year #3
+ $15.05	Interest Charge for Year #3
$140.49	Balance Owed at End of Year #3

NOTES:

Year #4:

$140.49	Balance from Year #3
× 12%	Interest Rate for Year #4
$16.86	Interest Charge for Year #4

$140.49	Principal for Year #4
+ $16.86	Interest Charge for Year #4
$157.35	Balance Owed at End of Year #4

Year #5:

$157.35	Balance from Year #4
× 12%	Interest Rate for Year #5
$18.88	Interest Charge for Year #5

$157.35	Principal for Year #5
+ $18.88	Interest Charge for Year #5
$176.23	Balance Owed at End of Year #5

Though this example does not seem dramatic, it does show how the compounding effect starts to increase the amount of interest you have to pay from one period to the next. By adding the previous interest charges onto the principal balance from the previous period and carrying that new total forward to the next period as the new principal balance, your interest charges go up with each compounding period.

Notice that the interest charge for Year #1 was only $12, but the interest charge for Year #5 was $18.88. We're not talking about huge amounts of money here, but the effect can be surprisingly large over time.

One of the ways that this compounding effect can have a major impact on you is that a compounding period is not always one year. For example, what would happen if in the above example, a compounding period was one month? The annual interest rate stays the same, but the interest compounds every month during that year.

When a compounding period is not the same length of time as the stated interest rate covers, we have to figure out what the interest rate is per compounding period.

For example, using our example of 12% per year, let's say that interest is compounded monthly. That means we will have to figure out what our interest rate is each month. Well, the reason I used a 12% annual interest rate is to make this very simple:

12%	Interest Per Year
÷ 12	Compounding Periods Per Year (Months)
= 1%	Interest Rate Per Compounding Period (Month)

That means instead of multiplying the principal amount by 12% one time, you have to multiply the principal amount by 1%, add that 1% to the principal amount, then multiply that total by 1% to get the second month's interest, etc. Here's how it looks:

$100.00	Beginning Principal Borrowed
+ $1.00	First Month's Interest Charge ($100 × 1%)
$101.00	New Principal Balance after Month #1
+ $1.01	Second Month's Interest Charge ($101 × 1%)
$102.01	New Principal Balance after Month #2
+ $1.02	Third Month's Interest Charge ($102.01 × 1%)
$103.03	New Principal Balance after Month #3
+ 1.03	Fourth Month's Interest Charge ($103.03 × 1%)
$104.06	New Principal Balance after Month #4
+ $1.04	Fifth Month's Interest Charge ($104.06 × 1%)
$105.10	New Principal Balance after Month #5

(continued from previous page...)

$105.10	New Principal Balance after Month #5
+ $1.05	Sixth Month's Interest Charge ($105.10 × 1%)
$106.15	New Principal Balance after Month #6
+ $1.06	Seventh Month's Interest Charge ($106.15 × 1%)
$107.21	New Principal Balance after Month #7
+ $1.07	Eighth Month's Interest Charge ($107.21 × 1%)
$108.28	New Principal Balance after Month #8
+ $1.08	Ninth Month's Interest Charge ($108.28 × 1%)
$109.36	New Principal Balance after Month #9
+ $1.09	Tenth Month's Interest Charge ($109.36 × 1%)
$110.45	New Principal Balance after Month #10
+ $1.10	Eleventh Month's Interest Charge ($110.45 × 1%)
$111.55	New Principal Balance after Month #11
+ $1.12	Twelfth Month's Interest Charge ($111.55 × 1%)
$112.67	New Principal Balance after Month #12

A couple of observations are important here. First of all, the total due at the end of the year was higher compounding monthly than it was compounding yearly. This may seem like a lot of work for the extra $0.67 we got from compounding monthly, but it showed the effect of breaking up a certain length of time into more compounding periods.

The other thing I want you to see is that each month, the interest charge was slightly higher. In this example the difference is very small, but the concept is very powerful, as you will see.

If we compare simple interest with compound interest in an example with more money and more time involved, you can see the difference that compounding the interest really makes.

As I mentioned before, simple interest, the way I presented it for purposes of explaining the compounding effect, may require that the interest be paid every time it comes due. If not, the interest might have to be added to the principal due and this would result in compounding, or paying interest on interest borrowed rather than paid when due.

However, the way these terms are used can vary, and just because something is referred to as a "simple interest loan" doesn't mean that you're not going to pay any compound interest. It really depends on how repayment of the loan is structured. The main point was to show how compound interest works – how interest can be paid on top of interest, as interest accumulates.

Let's say for purposes of comparison that we're going to borrow $1,000 and not make any payments for 30 years. Let's compare a simple interest loan with a compound interest loan at 12% interest, compounded monthly.

Simple Interest	Compound Interest	
$1,000.00	$1,000.00	Principal Borrowed
$120	$126.83	Interest: Year #1
$120	$142.91	Interest: Year #2
$120	$161.03	Interest: Year #3
$120	$181.46	Interest: Year #4
$120	$204.47	Interest: Year #5
$120	$230.40	Interest: Year #6
$120	$259.62	Interest: Year #7
$120	$292.55	Interest: Year #8
$120	$329.66	Interest: Year #9
$120	$371.46	Interest: Year #10
$120	$418.57	Interest: Year #11
$120	$471.66	Interest: Year #12
$120	$531.47	Interest: Year #13
$120	$598.88	Interest: Year #14
$120	$674.83	Interest: Year #15

$120	$760.42	Interest: Year #16
$120	$856.86	Interest: Year #17
$120	$965.53	Interest: Year #18
$120	$1,087.98	Interest: Year #19
$120	$1,225.96	Interest: Year #20
$120	$1,381.45	Interest: Year #21
$120	$1,556.65	Interest: Year #22
$120	$1,754.08	Interest: Year #23
$120	$1,976.53	Interest: Year #24
$120	$2,227.21	Interest: Year #25
$120	$2,509.67	Interest: Year #26
$120	$2,827.96	Interest: Year #27
$120	$3,186.62	Interest: Year #28
$120	$3,590.76	Interest: Year #29
$120	$4,046.16	Interest: Year #30
$4,600	**$35,949.64**	**Total Owed**

Notice that we start with the same loan amount, the same length of time and the same interest rate. The only difference is whether or not we compound the interest. With compound interest we owe $31,349.64 more than with simple interest. And we only borrowed $1,000 to begin with!

Now, that's dramatic. Due to compounding alone, we owe almost eight times as much as we did using the simple interest loan! Now we're starting to see how the effects of compound interest really add up over time, right?

The good news is that it's your choice whether you are going to allow compound interest to be used against you or if you're going to use compound interest to your advantage. Let's look at how you can use it to your advantage.

Let's say, for example, that you have decided to save $250/month starting at age 25 until you retire at age 65, for a total of 40 years. We're going to disregard any tax implications for this example, of course. I just want you to see how compound interest has a growing effect with each additional compounding period.

Let's use an interest rate of 10% per year, compounded monthly. Here's how the numbers will add up over time:

NOTES:

Year #1:	$3,141.39	Year #21:	$212,862.56
Year #2:	$6,611.73	Year #22:	$238,293.44
Year #3:	$10,445.46	Year #23:	$266,387.27
Year #4:	$14,680.62	Year #24:	$297,422.90
Year #5:	$19,359.27	Year #25:	$331,708.35
Year #6:	$24,527.83	Year #26:	$369,583.94
Year #7:	$30,237.60	Year #27:	$411,425.60
Year #8:	$36,545.27	Year #28:	$457,648.63
Year #9:	$43,513.43	Year #29:	$508,711.81
Year #10:	$51,211.25	Year #30:	$565,121.98
Year #11:	$59,715.12	Year #31:	$627,439.03
Year #12:	$69,109.47	Year #32:	$696,281.49
Year #13:	$79,487.53	Year #33:	$772,332.65
Year #14:	$90,952.30	Year #34:	$856,347.36
Year #15:	$103,617.59	Year #35:	$949,159.51
Year #16:	$117,609.09	Year #36:	$1,051,690.31
Year #17:	$133,065.69	Year #37:	$1,164,957.42
Year #18:	$150,140.80	Year #38:	$1,290,085.08
Year #19:	$169,003.90	Year #39:	$1,428,315.23
Year #20:	$189,842.21	Year #40:	$1,581,019.90

There are a couple of observations that are important to make here. First of all, you only deposited $120,000 of your own money here ($250 × 12 months × 40 years). But you earned $1,461,019.90 in interest! That's the power of compound interest.

Your interest rate was 10% per year – a tenth of the amount you deposit. But because of the number of compounding periods, you earned over twelve times as much interest as the amount of your own money that you deposited into this account! That's huge! And if you have consumer debt, this power is being used against you – not to your benefit.

If you can get out from under your consumer debt and start making this incredible power work for you instead of against you, you can accumulate large amounts of money where it might have been impossible otherwise.

There's another observation that I want to make sure we don't miss from this example. I also address this later in this workbook, but it is a very important part of understanding the long-term effects of compound interest, so I want to make sure to point it out here as well.

We used a long compounding period for this example, 40 years. It is very easy to postpone saving for retirement because we don't feel that the amount we can contribute right now will make much of a difference.

I do want to point out that postponing savings because you're working the plan in taught in this book is different from just postponing doing anything. This book will hopefully have you on a plan to get out from under your debt first, then save larger amounts for retirement afterwards. It's all part of trading your debt for wealth. It's hard to make compound interest work for you very effectively while it's still working hard against you.

Anyway, I used a 40-year example because I want to illustrate the long-term effects of compound interest. So, what would happen if at age 25 you say to yourself, "Self, I'm having too much fun right now to contribute to a retirement plan. There's no harm in waiting one year, right?"

After all, $250 per month for 1 year at 10% interest compounded monthly only adds up to $3,141.39, right? That's what it says in the chart above. So, if you can spare $3,141.39 out of that whopping sum of over $1.5 million, you should be able to postpone saving for a year, right?

Well, as you might have guessed, it doesn't work that way. Because of the long-term effects of compound interest, the difference is much more dramatic than that.

It might seem that you're only losing your principal and interest for the first year by not contributing for that first year, but it's really the last year that you lose, not the first year.

If you don't contribute the first year in this example, the next year becomes your first year. Then you only have 39 years. The amount you have in this example after 39 years is $1,428,315.23. That's still a healthy sum. But it is $152,704.67 less than you would have after 40 years.

That means that procrastinating for that one year didn't cost you a mere $3,141.39 of your retirement savings – it cost you $152,704.67! That's right. The long-term effects of compound interest are such that by your procrastinating one single year, your account balance is reduced by over $150,000.

I'm not trying to make you feel bad if you don't have 40 years to save for retirement. Most of us don't have that long. Even if you're 25 years old right now, there may be good reasons to postpone saving.

The best example would be if you're pursuing more education that will result in a higher income after completing your program. That may make it impossible to save for retirement right now. Education is a great investment that would justify postponing your retirement savings. And it can help you to save a higher monthly amount later so that you can more than make up for starting later than you might like.

I just want to make sure that you see the long-term effects of compound interest. It's your choice how you choose to use this knowledge, but it is important to be armed with this information when you go about making financial decisions.

You may not be surprised to hear that many people spend over $250/month in interest charges on their consumer debt. Looking at the numbers above, can you think of anything more effective to do with $250/month than to spend it servicing consumer debt? I thought so.

Here's another example to think about. Let's say that you just found a great sale on a LCD TV and you've been craving one for a long time. You have all the TVs you need, but you're really dying for one that nice. You have the money and it's yours to spend. I'm not going to tell you that you should or should not buy the TV, but it's good to be able to make an informed decision, right?

Okay. So there's an awesome TV that's normally $2,000 and it's on a huge blowout sale for half price – only $1,000! Wow, that sounds like a great investment, right? After all, if you don't buy that one now, you're just going to wind up spending more when you buy one later, right?

Well, let's say that you're 30 years old and you plan to retire at age 70. You won't need all your money at age 70 – your retirement accounts can continue to grow because you're not going to spend it all at once, but let's just say that you want to see how much money you could have at age 70 by sacrificing your plans to buy a $1,000 TV right now.

Let's use a more conservative interest rate this time – 8% per year, compounded monthly. I'll make this short and only show every five years:

Year #5:	$1,489.85	Year #25:	$7,340.18
Year #10:	$2,219.64	Year #30:	$10,935.73
Year #15:	#3,306.92	Year #35:	$16,292.55
Year # 20:	$4,926.80	Year #40:	$24,273.39

Remember that we're using a more conservative rate of interest and that this is only a one-time $1,000 sum, not a monthly contribution. But even so, the long-term effects of compound interest make this a pretty sizable amount of money after 40 years.

Like I said before, whether you decide to spend the money or invest it is up to you. There will be times when spending money to enjoy life is the right decision. It's just good to know what your options are and what the long-term effects of your decisions will be so that you can make the best decisions possible.

For those of you who would like to do some math, here are some optional problems for you to solve:

---

1) If you start at age 35 and put $300/month into a retirement account paying 8% interest compounded annually, how much will you have in your account at age 65?

2) Suppose you start at age 25 instead of age 35 – how much will you have in your retirement account at age 65?

3) Suppose you were to inherit $50,000. You are tempted to buy a boat but you are only 25 years old and the attorney told you that if you invest wisely you could retire on what this inheritance could become over time. If you invested this sum at 8% compounded annually, what will it be in 40 years?

4) What if you were able to get a 12% return over the same 40 years?

Notes:

STEP #2

COMMIT TO LIVING DEBT-FREE

At this moment, you may not yet have the motivation to commit to living a debt-free lifestyle. However, by the time you have finished this course, you should not only have the motivation, but also the skills and the drive necessary to make this a permanent change in your life.

When you can see clearly how living without debt can dramatically improve your life, and also see exactly how to go about accomplishing this goal in a very reasonable period of time, I believe that your life will be changed forever.

There are many reasons to adopt a debt-free lifestyle and stick with it permanently. Here are just a few:

Reason #1: Paying interest on purchases severely limits how much you can purchase. Because you wind up paying a lot more for your purchase in the long run, you cannot afford to purchase as much.

Reason #2: In many cases, the interest you pay on your purchases could be used to completely finance your retirement. That's right. For many of you, if you were to completely exchange your interest-paying lifestyle for a debt-free, interest-receiving lifestyle, and invest the money that you saved, you could retire on that alone.

Reason #3: People who use credit cards for their purchases spend approximately twice as much as those who do not. This is largely because of impulse buying. People who pay cash for their purchases actually think about whether or not they can afford or really need the item before spending their money on it.

Reason #4: If you have cash, you can sometimes get a better deal on your purchase than when using credit. You may also be more motivated to shop around before spending your money. When you understand what a difference each dollar can make in the long run, you will be more careful to find the right price for an item, instead of buying impulsively just because it has a "low monthly payment".

Reason #5: Financial planners recommend having an emergency fund of between three and six months living expenses, depending upon how varied and dependable your sources of income. This money, in order to be safe and quickly accessible, earns a very low rate of interest. If your living expenses are cut in half due to lack of debt, more of your savings can be put into investments that earn higher returns. This, of course, means more money in your pocket.

Reason #6: If you were to suffer a life-altering event, such as loss of an income source, or just needed a less stressful (lower-paying) job, you could deal with that occurrence without having to sell your home or make other lifestyle changes that might be very uncomfortable. You simply would not require as much income to maintain your lifestyle if your have no debt.

Reason #7: Debt causes stress. I don't think I need to tell you how many fights get started between husbands and wives because of excessive debt. Financial problems are probably the #1 leading cause of divorce. And even those who stay together often waste much of their life worrying and arguing about money, instead of enjoying the relationships they value above all their possessions. A debt-free lifestyle will add happiness to your life and relationships, and reduce stress and frustration.

Reason #8: Living debt-free allows you the freedom to live your life the way you choose to instead of being a slave to your debts. Making choices based on what you want out of life, instead of working at a job that you hate or making other compromises with your life to accommodate your debts, is really the only way to live. Don't you agree?

List 3 ways that living debt-free can improve *your* life:

(1)

(2)

(3)

Notes:

Cut Up Those Credit Cards !!

Even if you're not ready to do this just yet, by the time you've finished this workbook you should be ready and anxious to get rid of those credit cards. I know this is a difficult thing to do, but it will pay you well in the long run.

You are probably wondering how you will function in our modern society without credit cards. First of all, I need to point out that credit cards do not exist to improve your life. Credit cards exist to make money for the credit card companies. The unsuspecting public has fallen into a trap by giving into the temptation to "buy now and pay later". This trap will rob us of attaining financial independence unless we can escape.

Even so, I am well aware that our society revolves around the use of credit cards and you may be nervous about giving them up. Here's how you can be rid of those wealth-stealing credit cards, without missing them too much:

First, realize that you do not really need a *credit* card in order to make hotel reservations, phone purchases, etc. I have a VISA Check Card, and it is accepted just like any other VISA card. I use it routinely to buy gas, go out to dinner, make phone purchases, buy airline tickets, make hotel reservations, etc.

A *Debit Card* or a *Check Card* can be used as if it were a regular credit card, but you never receive a bill. Your purchase is deducted from your checking account as if you had written a check. So when the gas station doesn't accept personal checks, or you need to make a purchase over the phone, you can pull out the plastic just like anyone else.

Let me make a suggestion though. Keep your debit or check card with your checkbook and every time you use the card, record the purchase in your check register as soon as possible. This will help you remember that you are paying for your purchase, not charging it. This is also necessary so that you don't forget to deduct the amount from your checking account balance.

Also, when you are using your card, imagine that you are handing over cash for your purchase, and if you wouldn't pay cash, then don't use the card. Old habits die hard and if you're not careful, you could still fall into "plastic over-spending". Remember that the amount you just put on your card will probably be deducted from your checking account the next business day.

Second, after you have completed this workbook you should realize that you will not actually be giving anything up by getting rid of your credit cards. You will simply be avoiding the "instant gratification" trap in order to become able to afford a lot more than you can now. Your money will go a lot further when you're living debt-free.

2012 Note: Okay – Maybe Just One

Okay, okay. I'm revising this book 14 years after its original writing, and I have to agree with you that in 2012 it doesn't seem normal to not have a credit card. There may be limitations on how much you can charge per day on a debit card, and you do get better fraud protection from a credit card than you do from a debit card.

So, I suggest having one and only one credit card – and pay the balance in full every month no later than the due date. Remember – the credit card companies are not in business to provide you with great service at a reasonable price. They are in business to make as much money as they possibly can off of you, and they resort to sneaky, slimy tactics to do so. Their over-the-limit fees and late fees are downright abusive. And their ability to raise interest rates on you on balances you're already carrying with them is just plain wrong.

There are so many things they do to deceitfully bilk money out of their customers that I can't go into in this book. Just consider yourself warned – you should look at your credit card company as if it were a pickpocket wandering the streets looking for a wallet to steal. And if it sounds like I really hate credit card companies – good!

I should acknowledge that there is some new legislation that is starting to crack down on some of the abuses that credit card companies have inflicted upon the unsuspecting public. Hopefully, this will help to make the use of credit cards less perilous than it has been in the past.

I should also add that if you're trying to obtain credit, paying down your credit card balances always looks good – but closing the accounts may not be the best idea until after you've obtained the credit you need. Your credit rating may be affected by the amount of available credit you are presently utilizing. That means if your balance is $2,000 out of $10,000 available, that will look a lot better than if your balance is $2,000 out of $2,500 available.

Unfortunately, in the short time between the first writing of this workbook and its most current revision, we have moved to a more credit and credit card dependent society, and now it does not appear to be an option to just avoid credit altogether. We must now learn how to work within the system and understand how to use credit without letting credit use us.

The New American Emergency Fund

If your emergency fund consists of a credit card that's not yet charged up to its limit, you may not be able to cut up all of your credit cards today. But you should work towards achieving the goal of having them all paid off as quickly as possible. If this is your situation, here's what I suggest:

(1)   Choose one credit card with an adequate amount of unused credit limit to cover your average emergency, and set it aside.

(2)   Cut up all the others and close the accounts. [Note: Again, closing the accounts may affect your credit score, so if you need to keep some of them open temporarily, do so carefully. Remember the fees and temptations involved with having consumer credit readily available.]

(3)   Include the card you set aside with the others in your **Rapid-Debt-Payoff** plan, which we will discuss shortly.

(4)   Put your "emergency" credit card someplace where it is "inconveniently accessible". This could be a safe-deposit box, a safe in your attic, in a glass of water you put in the freezer, whatever. (Just don't lose it.) If it is too easy to access, it could be tempting.

(5)   Only use the card in case of a legitimate emergency (not a fashion emergency).

(6)   Get a debit card or check card to use when it is not possible or practical to pay by check.

(7)   As soon as you are able to establish and fund a real emergency account, use this one last credit card with wisdom, keeping the balance paid in full and only using the card for purchases that you are willing to pay cash for. As I stated earlier, I do realize that nowadays, there are a few legitimate reasons to have a credit card. I do think it's a good idea to have *one* – if you can control your spending and pay the balance in full every month.

(8)   Use the other concepts taught in this book so that you will never need or want to depend on consumer debt or abuse credit cards again!

List three ways your life could improve if you gave up credit cards?

1.

2.

3.

STEP #3

FIND YOUR ACCELERATOR

I don't mean the accelerator in your car, but the idea is the same. The **Accelerator**, just like the one in your car, is the thing that makes you go faster. In this case it's not driving speed we're talking about; it's total-debt-elimination speed.

The concepts you are about to learn will work, with or without an accelerator. But when you see the dramatic effect that adding an accelerator will have on your plan, you will definitely want to turbo-charge your plan with the largest accelerator you can find.

We will actually go through this process before learning the rest of the plan, in order to keep the steps in order. If you want to, you can go through this step again after you've learned how to put a plan together, as you may be motivated to increase your accelerator after learning how much it can benefit your plan.

What exactly is your *accelerator*? It's the extra amount of money that you can set aside each month to accelerate your debt-payoff. Remember that your goal is to have all your debts paid off as quickly as possible so that the money you were spending "servicing" your debt can be used to accomplish other goals, such as building wealth. This is literally "trading debt for wealth".

Of course, it is important that you stay out of debt once you have gotten out of debt. This system cannot work properly unless you adopt a debt-free lifestyle, because using the principle of compound interest to your advantage instead of allowing it to be used against you, is where the money will come from to accomplish your financial goals.

As I mentioned earlier, it is possible to implement this system effectively without an accelerator. But the long-term results when using an accelerator are substantially improved; enough to motivate you to find your accelerator, and as big a one as you can.

If you find yourself significantly more motivated to use an accelerator after you've completed this course than you are now, then you will want to go through this section again, in order to possibly find an even larger accelerator than you might have the first time through.

NOTES:

MAKING A BUDGET

The first place to look for your accelerator is in your family budget. You may know off the top of your head that you can afford "X" number of dollars each month to accelerate your **Rapid-Debt-Payoff** program, or you may not have any idea how much you can afford. You may even be absolutely positive that you cannot afford anything as your accelerator for this program. Whatever your situation, don't worry. For now, just go through the steps. I believe you will be pleased with the results.

The idea of making a budget is not usually appealing. I'm aware of that. But this is not designed to restrict you and make you feel rationed. I want you to make a budget so that you can see where all your money is going, to help you identify if there are funds that you would rather use more productively, in order to improve your life.

The budget sheet that I have included will specify all your sources of income, categorize all your expenditures, and then see what's leftover (or what's not). If you already have a budgeting system, and you like it better than the one included here, that's okay. Use whatever works for you.

Notice on the budget sheet that follows, that income sources are listed first, then fixed expenses, then variable expenses, then the positive or negative amount left over. You write in the amount that you budget for each category or item, then the amounts actually spent per week so you can compare. This way you can adjust the amount that you budget for an item, to keep it realistic.

The purpose here is to look at where your money is going and see if some changes can be made, to come up with the largest accelerator possible. By putting everything in writing, you will be able decide how much you are willing to spend on what, and then purposefully go about sticking with what you have decided. If you know *why* you are going to intentionally restrict you spending temporarily, it's easier to stick with it.

For example, let's say that you have decided that you are only willing to spend "X" number of dollars on lunches per month so that you can afford the accelerator you have chosen. Keeping track of how much you are spending, you notice that you are going to have to take your lunch from home for one week in order to meet your goal. Knowing why you are doing this will make it much more likely that you will actually do it. Without a purpose, you will probably just eat out and not pay any attention to how much it costs you in a month.

As you go through the budget page that follows, use a pencil so that you can change the numbers until they fit correctly and give you the results you want. Be sure to be realistic. You won't stick with it unless you believe it is possible and not too unpleasant.

Go ahead and look over the following budget sheet, then read the instructions found immediately afterwards. I have included three budget sheets so that you can write on one now and have extras to use later or make copies with, in case you would like to use this on a monthly basis.

Notes:

Income: (1) $_____ (2) $_____ Total: _____

Description	Budget	Week 1	Week 2	Week 3	Week 4	Total	Excess
Fixed Expenses:							
Mortgage/Rent							
Car Payment #1							
Car Payment #2							
Student Loans							
Life Insurance							
Auto Insurance							
Day Care							
Child Supp./Alim.							
Other:							
Other:							
Variable Expenses:							
Groceries							
Electricity							
Natural Gas							
Telephone							
Water/Trash							
Cable/Satellite TV							
Church/Charities							
Gasoline							
Auto Expenses							
Dry Cleaning							
Entertainment							
Kids' Allowance							
Haircuts							
Lunches							
Pocket Money							
Emergency Savings							
Savings for Goal:							
Other:							
Revolving Charge:							
Visa							
MasterCard							
Furniture:							
Appliance:							
Other:							
Other:							
Non-Monthly Acct:							
Insurance:							
Property Tax							
Clothing							
Gifts/Holidays							
Home Improvement							

Income: $_____ **Less Expenses:** $_____   **My *ACCELERATOR*:**

Equals Discretionary Income: $_____ $_____

Income: (1) $_____ (2) $_____ **Total:** _____

Description	Budget	Week 1	Week 2	Week 3	Week 4	Total	Excess
Fixed Expenses:							
Mortgage/Rent							
Car Payment #1							
Car Payment #2							
Student Loans							
Life Insurance							
Auto Insurance							
Day Care							
Child Supp./Alim.							
Other:							
Other:							
Variable Expenses:							
Groceries							
Electricity							
Natural Gas							
Telephone							
Water/Trash							
Cable/Satellite TV							
Church/Charities							
Gasoline							
Auto Expenses							
Dry Cleaning							
Entertainment							
Kids' Allowance							
Haircuts							
Lunches							
Pocket Money							
Emergency Savings							
Savings for Goal:							
Other:							
Revolving Charge:							
Visa							
MasterCard							
Furniture:							
Appliance:							
Other:							
Other:							
Non-Monthly Acct:							
Insurance:							
Property Tax							
Clothing							
Gifts/Holidays							
Home Improvement							

Income: $_____ **Less Expenses:** $_____   **My ACCELERATOR:**

Equals Discretionary Income: $_____ $_____

Income: (1) $_____ (2) $_____ **Total:** _____

Description	Budget	Week 1	Week 2	Week 3	Week 4	Total	Excess
Fixed Expenses:							
Mortgage/Rent							
Car Payment #1							
Car Payment #2							
Student Loans							
Life Insurance							
Auto Insurance							
Day Care							
Child Supp./Alim.							
Other:							
Other:							
Variable Expenses:							
Groceries							
Electricity							
Natural Gas							
Telephone							
Water/Trash							
Cable/Satellite TV							
Church/Charities							
Gasoline							
Auto Expenses							
Dry Cleaning							
Entertainment							
Kids' Allowance							
Haircuts							
Lunches							
Pocket Money							
Emergency Savings							
Savings for Goal:							
Other:							
Revolving Charge:							
Visa							
MasterCard							
Furniture:							
Appliance:							
Other:							
Other:							
Non-Monthly Acct:							
Insurance:							
Property Tax							
Clothing							
Gifts/Holidays							
Home Improvement							

Income: $_____ **Less Expenses:** $_____   **My *ACCELERATOR*:**
Equals Discretionary Income: $_____ $_____

Instructions for Budget Sheet

The budget sheet you just looked over is designed to help you to find your accelerator. It can also be used as your monthly budgeting sheet if you so desire. Keep a spare sheet unmarked if you would like to make copies for future months. As long as you purchased this book legally, you have my permission to make copies of the budget sheet for your own, personal use.

Here's how to use the budget sheet:

(1)   At the top of the page, list all your sources of income and each monthly income amount. Enter the total monthly income to the right.

(2)   In the "Budget" column, write in the monthly amounts for all of your *fixed expenses*. These amounts will be easy to obtain because they are the same every month.

(3)   Still in the "Budget" column, write in your "budgeted" amount for each of your *variable expenses*. These amounts should be your realistic estimate of what each item or category will cost every month if you are careful.

Base these amounts on your records of previous expenditures, or estimates where there is no record. The amounts you chose should not be higher than is reasonably necessary, and should not be lower than is realistic for you to stick with it.

(4)   Continuing in the "Budget" column, enter your **current minimum payment** for each revolving charge and credit card amount. Even if you pay more every month, enter the minimum payment. The difference will become part of your *accelerator*, so it will still be going towards paying off your debts. It's just that we want to make this process as efficient as possible.

Next, still in the "Budget" column, fill in the amount you will need to set aside per month to pay for *non-monthly expenditures*. You should probably have at least one separate bank account for these non-emergency, non-monthly expenses.

For example, let's say that your family spends $1,800 per year for Christmas gifts and holiday expenses. Unless you have a reliable Christmas bonus to cover this expense, you should be depositing $150 per month into this account to cover these expenses. The same concept applies to any other items in this category that apply to your situation.

(5)   Now, add up the total of everything you listed in the "Budget" column. Compare this number with the "Total Income" you listed in the top right-hand corner. Depending on how much the difference is, you may want to go back and

make some adjustments in the areas that you have some control over. These will usually be the *Variable Expenses* and some of the *Non-Monthly* items.

The totals can be compared at the bottom, left-hand corner of the budget sheet. The amount you have left over is called *discretionary income*. If you have a deficit, steps will have to be taken to correct this problem.

Maintaining a monthly deficit will often cause a downward spiral towards bankruptcy. It should be dealt with as quickly as possible so that you can proceed with this program and meet your financial goals. Some suggestions will follow shortly and others can be found in the *Misc.* section at the end of this book.

If you are just breaking even, that is, not operating at a deficit, but not presently able to find your accelerator, do not be discouraged. This system will still work, and you need to start immediately. Do *not* take on any more debt, and be very careful with your expenses.

Use the budget sheet every month and remember that small amounts do make a difference. An extra $20 per month means that you can get ahead, and a deficit of $20 per month can shut you down. There's a fine line between progress and trouble.

(6)   When you are satisfied with your Discretionary Income amount, choose how much of this you want to set aside each month and designate as your Accelerator. It doesn't necessarily have to be the whole amount, but you will enjoy a bigger advantage with a larger accelerator.

(7)   In the four columns to the right of the Budget column, enter the amounts spent each week for each item or category. The fixed expenses and other monthly bills will usually be easy. Just enter the monthly payment in the week that you paid it.

There will usually be a few extra days before Week 1 and/or after Week 4. Just include them in week 1 or 4, as appropriate. The only reason this budget is divided into weeks is so you can see how you're doing and make any necessary adjustments as you go along.

For example, if you can see on paper that you've used up most of your Lunch budget after the second week, you may decide to take your lunch for a week instead of eating out. The motivation of meeting your goal can help you stay within your budget, if you keep track of your expenses so you know how you're doing.

The level of sacrifice you are willing to make in order to reach your financial goals is completely up to you. I won't try to tell you what's right or what's wrong for you. You need to construct a program you can live with, or you won't stick with it. Realize, however, that some relatively easy sacrifices today can make your dreams come true tomorrow.

(8)   The two columns at the far right are simply to add up what you spent in each category for weeks 1 through 4, and compare to what was budgeted. You can use this information to make adjustments in your budgeted amount or to alter your spending habits as you go along, whichever is appropriate.

What parts of your budget could be adjusted to help you meet your financial goals?

Notes:

Other Places to "Find Your Accelerator"

There are many ways to find a little extra money each month, and a little will go a long way in this program. Here are a few suggestions:

(1)   Give up a vice. Quit smoking or some other expensive habit that's not good for you anyway.

(2)   Trim your entertainment budget by replacing an expensive dinner with a picnic, a walk in the park, a game of tennis, etc. My wife and I enjoy going for coffee and checking out books at the local Barnes & Noble. There are inexpensive ways to enjoy getting out of the house.

(3)   Get a better deal on your life insurance. Many of you would be better off with an inexpensive *term* policy instead of an overpriced cash-value policy. Shop term rates and get the best one for the right policy.

(4)   Buy a two-year-old car instead of a new one. You can get one in great condition and save a fortune. That expensive new car is used anyway, by the time you get it home.

(5)   Take your lunch to work. Lunches in restaurants really add up.

(6)   Go to the afternoon movie and sneak in your own snacks. You'll save more than you might think, especially with the kids. (I accept no responsibility if you get caught ☺)

(7)   Split an appetizer and one entrée. My wife and I do this all the time.

(8)   Work two hours of overtime per week, if it's available. You'll hardly notice the difference, and this alone could be your accelerator.

(9)   Start taking your spouse on dates centered around physical exercise, instead of eating and entertainment. You'll save money and feel better too.

(10)   Rob a convenience store. (Please don't! I'm just checking to see if you're still awake.)

(10)   (Seriously now) Get a better deal on your auto insurance. Sometimes there's a reputable company that can save you money by doing it over the phone. Also, be careful not to duplicate coverages with your homeowners or health insurance policies. It's easy to throw money away on duplicate coverage if you're not careful.

(11)   Sell something you don't use anyway. How about a garage sale?

(12)   Start a part-time, home based business doing something you enjoy. See if you can get paid for working on a hobby.

(13)   Look for *non-qualified* (no penalty for withdrawal) savings funds that may be able to be used to jump-start your program and create a positive cash flow. Though the accelerator is generally spoken of as a monthly amount, any lump-sum that is available can reduce your monthly requirement, creating a positive cash flow and, therefore, an accelerator.

Don't completely use up an emergency fund. Keep enough to be safe. Also, don't use *qualified* funds if there's any way around it.   The penalties make it unattractive. (Qualified funds are retirement funds that have penalties for early withdrawal and become taxable income when withdrawn. It's usually best to leave those funds in a qualified account unless it's an emergency.)

If you choose this option, continue through the workbook and prioritize your debts before paying anything off. Pay them off *in order*, until your chosen amount is exhausted. The amount of the payments you will no longer have to make every month will become your accelerator. Do not take on any more debt, or you have just wasted your savings, and that is not what you're trying to accomplish.

There are many other ideas that you can use to find your accelerator, but this list will start you thinking. Use what works for you.

One thing I really want to make clear here is this: This program is not supposed to make you feel financially claustrophobic. These ideas are just to help you think of some things that you might want to do to speed up the process of getting completely out of debt, so you can start building wealth for retirement, or working towards other financial goals. You do not have to pinch every penny you can get your hands on in order to make this system work. Design a program that you will stick with.

When you have finished working through the budget page, and have determined the amount of your accelerator, you are ready to proceed with putting together your very own, personal, Rapid-Debt-Payoff program. Get ready to see some fabulous results as you implement your program.

List 3 ways that you can improve your accelerator:

(1)

(2)

(3)

Notes:

Notes:

STEP #4

YOUR "RAPID-DEBT-PAYOFF" PROGRAM

You may be thinking, "Rapid-Debt-Payoff? That's easy for you to say. I can hardly keep up!" Believe me, I understand. There is a specific principle I want to show you, that can help you get out of debt much more quickly than you ever thought possible. People have used this technique to get *completely* out of debt – including their home – in less than half the time that they were scheduled to be out of debt, often within seven years or less. Yes, this method really works!

Warning! This method requires *self-discipline*, another very unpopular concept today.

The best way to explain how this **Rapid-Debt-Payoff** concept works is with an example. Let's suppose that Mr. and Mrs. Jones and their children make up the typical American family – middle class income and up to their eyeballs in debt.

Here's a look at the Jones's debt situation (and there are a lot of people "keeping up with the Joneses"):

Description of Debt	Min. Monthly Payment	Interest Rate	Principal Balance	Estimated Time to Payoff
House (P & I)	$ 950.00	9%	$ 116,378	28 years 0 months
Car #1	400.00	10%	12,396	3 years 0 months
Car #2	350.00	10%	5,828	1 year 6 months
Furniture Pmt.	280.00	19%	2,332	9 months
Dept. Store #1	140.00	20%	2,800	(when h--- freezes)
Dept. Store #2	85.00	20%	1,700	(same as above)
Credit Card #1	195.00	21%	4,875	(same as above)
Credit Card #2	140.00	19%	3,500	(same as above)
Credit Card #3	95.00	20%	2,100	(same as above)
Credit Card #4	65.00	21%	1,400	(same as above)

The Jones family spends $2,700 per month "servicing their debt" (or being "serviced" by their debt, you could say). Many families have much more debt than this, and some have less. As home prices and interest rates vary widely across time and location, your personal situation will probably be quite different; but this will serve as a good example for our purposes.

Let's say that in addition to servicing their debt, Mr. and Mrs. Jones can afford to put aside $150 per month, for an emergency fund and to save for retirement. They were planning to start saving immediately in a savings account at their local bank.

After Mr. and Mrs. Jones have listed all their debts, as shown above, the next thing they should do is *prioritize* them for *rapid-payoff*. What they need to do is put them in order, starting with the one that would be the quickest to pay off, then work their way down to the one which would take the longest time to pay off.

Before trying to determine the correct order in which to list the debts, first figure out how much extra money you can afford in your monthly budget, to help you pay off your debts early. You should already have completed this in the previous step.

The reason you need to know your *accelerator* before prioritizing your debts, is that your accelerator is part of the formula I devised to determine that priority. If your accelerator is "zero", don't worry. This system works even if you don't have any extra money to put towards your goal; it just works faster if you do.

If you can afford an extra $200 to $300 per month, you will see dramatic results fast. But if you can only add an extra $25 to $50 per month, this will help. Don't think that just because you can only afford an extra $25 per month, it won't make a difference. It *will* make a difference. Add whatever amount you can fit into your budget.

If you cannot add anything to what you are presently paying on your monthly debts, just plug in a zero any place it asks for your accelerator, and go through the steps. This will still work, and you will enjoy the results if you stick with it.

If you can't even make all your minimum payments now, and are considering bankruptcy, I will deal with your situation at the end of this workbook.

Back to our example. For Mr. and Mrs. Jones, let's assume that the only extra money they have that could assist them with their *Rapid-Debt-Payoff* program, is the $150 per month that they were about to start saving at the bank.

Let's change their plans a little. Let's say that $50 per month goes into an emergency fund at the bank. This is important. If you're trying to get out of debt, it can be very discouraging to have to take on more debt due to an unforeseen emergency. I suggest putting a small amount aside every month into a special savings account solely for emergency use.

As your accelerator grows (you will see how this happens shortly), the accelerator itself can function as an emergency fund, if necessary. However, this amount is not always accessible since you are using it every month to pay off debts. Unless you already have an emergency fund in place, I still recommend making a small monthly contribution to this account.

I do not usually recommend taking the time to first save up your entire *three to six months living expenses* before starting your Rapid-Debt-Payoff program, though it is important to have this amount as soon as possible. In many cases, by the time you can have this amount saved up while juggling all those debts, you could be completely out of debt. This may significantly reduce the amount you need in emergency savings.

Between the small monthly contribution you make to your emergency fund and the gradual reduction in the amount you will need (because your debts are being paid off so your monthly overhead is going down), you will be making progress toward having your full emergency fund. When your debts are all paid off, the amount you were using to pay off your debts will go toward completing your emergency fund, then into investments.

If you have an emergency fund now, that's wonderful. You may still want to contribute a small amount every month into this account, so that you have a method of replenishing the funds that are used for emergencies. If you have a very large emergency fund right now, you might consider using part of it to jump-start your debt acceleration program, by starting with a lump-sum payment. Keep enough to be safe.

Okay. The Joneses have started their emergency fund. How about the other $100 per month? Instead of saving this right now, we are going to use this $100 per month to help the Jones' Rapid-Debt-Payoff program. I'll show you in Step #5 how we are going to make up for this amount not going into savings at this time.

So, we've determined that Mr. and Mrs. Jones can put in an extra $100 per month above their current minimum monthly payments to help their Rapid-Debt-Payoff program. Remember that this will work even if you cannot afford to add any extra money to your current minimum monthly payment amount. It just works more quickly if you can.

Now let's help Mr. and Mrs. Jones to prioritize their debts. We will do this by determining how quickly each debt could be paid off, if we were to add that extra $100 per month to each specific bill. Then we will put them in order, the fastest one first. This is easy to do on a financial calculator, if you know how to do financial functions. However, because this book was written for non-financial professionals, I came up with a simple formula that is so easy, anyone can use it to quickly prioritize their debts.

Principal Balance Due / (Min. Payment + Accelerator) = Priority Index

Use this formula on each debt, adding the accelerator to each one separately, as if it were the only debt on your list. Let's go through an example. Credit Card #1 from the Jones's debt list on page 6 has a principal balance due of $4,875. The current minimum monthly payment is $195. The accelerator is the $100 we decided on earlier. The equation looks like this:

$$\$4,875 \ / \ (\$195 + \$100) \ =$$
$$4,875 \ / \ 295 \ =$$
$$16.5$$

The Priority Index number for Credit Card #1 is 16.5. When this calculation has been done for all the debts on the list, the Priority Index numbers are compared to each other and the debts are listed in order, from the lowest Priority Index number to the highest.

If two or more Priority Index numbers are exactly the same, or are extremely close, then look at their respective interest rates and put the one with the highest rate first. This is not necessary in the Jones example and can be considered a minor detail if it's the slightest bit confusing.

Let's take all the Jones's debts and do this step with them now. Here's what I get:

Description of Debt	Principal Balance	Minimum Payment	Accel- erator	Priority Index	Payoff Order
House Payment	116,378	950	100	110.8	10
Car #1	12,396	400	100	24.8	9
Car #2	5,828	350	100	13.0	6
Furniture	2,332	280	100	6.1	1
Dept. Store #1	2,800	140	100	11.7	5
Dept. Store #2	1,700	85	100	9.2	3
Credit Card #1	4,875	195	100	16.5	8
Credit Card #2	3,500	140	100	14.6	7
Credit Card #3	2,100	95	100	10.8	4
Credit Card #4	1,400	65	100	8.5	2

Please note that just because we added the accelerator into all the accounts listed above, that does not mean that that's the amount to be paid. This was only for the purpose of determining the Priority Index.

So, what's next? Well, here's where it gets interesting. Now that we know the amount of the Jones's accelerator, and have determined in what order to pay off the debts, we are ready to see how quickly these debts can be "paid-in-full".

Mr. and Mrs. Jones have current minimum monthly payments totaling $2,700 per month. Adding in the $100 accelerator that they will use to minimize their payoff time, Mr. and Mrs. Jones will be paying $2,800 per month until all their debts are paid in full.

It is important that the <u>current</u> minimum monthly payment be written down and used as the starting point for our payment strategy. If you pay only the minimum amount due each month, your bill can gradually go down, ensuring that it takes years and years to pay off your debt. Your creditors will benefit greatly from this, but you will not.

Another point that must be emphasized here is this: Don't put any more charges on those credit cards! Cut them up! Close the accounts! (Remember what I said earlier about this, of course.) We're trying to get *out* of debt. Especially if you are using funds that would otherwise be invested for retirement, you must be committed to *not* taking on more debt. This vicious cycle has to be stopped if you want to get ahead.

If you cannot commit to avoiding more debt, then *don't* use all your investable, discretionary income to accelerate your debt payoff. Put some away for retirement, and don't delay. No, you won't enjoy all the benefits of this program; but at least you'll have something set aside for your retirement.

_____

List one thing you've learned from this section so far:

_____

Okay. Let's fill in some blanks here and see how this system really works. First we'll list all the Jones's debts, in order of our intended payoff. Then we'll write in their Starting Payment, the Accelerator, the total payment to be made, and length of time it will take to pay off the debt in full.

	Description of Debt	Starting Payment		Accel- erator		Total Payment	New Time to Payoff
1)	Furniture	280	+	100	=	380	7 months
2)	Credit Card #4	65	+	380	=	445	3 months
3)	Dept. Store #2	85	+	445	=	530	3 months
4)	Credit Card #3	95	+	530	=	625	3 months
5)	Dept. Store #1	140	+	625	=	765	2 months
6)	Car #2	350	+	765	=	1115	(PAID)
7)	Credit Card #2	140	+	1115	=	1255	2 months
8)	Credit Card #1	195	+	1255	=	1450	2 months
9)	Car #1	400	+	1450	=	1850	3 months
10)	House	950	+	1850	=	2800	4 yrs. 1 mo.

Total Time to be Completely Debt-Free: 6 Years and 2 Months

I realize that this requires a detailed explanation. Here it is, line by line:

Line 1: The furniture debt is the first one that Mr. and Mrs. Jones will be paying off. The regular monthly payment is $280. We add to that the extra $100 that Mr. and Mrs. Jones are using to help accelerate their debt payoff, for a total monthly payment of $380. This amount will be paid every month until their furniture debt is paid in full. At this rate, the debt will be paid in 7 months.

Line 2: Credit Card #4 is the second debt the Joneses will be paying off. The starting payment is $65 per month. For their accelerator, Mr. and Mrs. Jones are no longer limited to $100. Since the furniture debt is now paid in full, they can use the entire $380 per month they were paying on the furniture bill as their extra amount. Adding this to the starting payment of $65, gives us a total monthly payment of $445. At this rate, Credit Card #4 will be paid off in 3 months. (That is, 3 months after the furniture debt is paid.)

Line 3: Dept. Store #2 is next. The Joneses have been paying $85 per month; but now that Credit Card #4 is paid off, they can add the $445 that was going to that bill onto the $85 they've been paying, for a total of $530 per month. At this rate, Dept. Store #2 will be paid off in 3 months.

Note: The total monthly amount the Joneses are paying on their debts has NOT increased. They simply "roll-over" the amount they were paying on one debt onto the next one, to accelerate their payoff.

Line 4: After paying off Dept. Store #2, there will be an extra $530 per month available to add to the $95 per month already being paid. At $625 per month, Credit Card #3 will be paid off in 3 months.

Line 5: After adding the $625 per month no longer needed for Credit Card #3 to the $140 already being paid, Dept. Store #1 will be paid off in 2 months.

Line 6: Car #2 will be paid off at the same time as Dept. Store #1, leaving $1,115 per month available to add to the next debt on the list.

Line 7: With a total payment of $1,255 per month, Credit Card #2 will be paid off in another 2 months.

Line 8: With the total payment now at $1,450 per month, Credit Card #1 will be paid off in 2 months after Credit Card #2.

Line 9: At $1,850 per month, Car #1 will be paid off just 3 months later.

Line 10: This is the grand finale. The Jones home will be completely paid for in just 4 years and 1 month. This is because the entire $2,800 per month can now be concentrated onto this one debt, accelerating their payoff and saving them a fortune in interest charges.

Like I said before, this is not magic. But the results can certainly make it look like it is.

In the example chart above, why does the *Accelerator* keep going up?

There are a couple of things that I should mention before we leave this section. First, the above example did not take into consideration that each time a *final payment* is made on one of these debts, the last payment is only a **partial payment.** In some cases, the final payment is significantly less than the monthly amount that was being paid at the time. If this leftover amount is applied to the next debt, the payoff time will be **even faster** than the example showed it to be!

Second, to come up with the payoff times, I had to use a financial calculator. Don't worry. Even if you don't use a financial calculator so you don't have exact payoff dates, you will see the momentum and be amazed at how quickly you are getting out of debt. Also, there are financial calculators online now that can make it very easy to get payoff times, etc.

Now let's compare the Jones' original scenario to the one we just prepared for them. When we first listed all of their debts, it looked like they would be lucky to ever be out of debt, didn't it? Now that we've put this plan in place for them, they will be completely out of debt in about 6 years.

Again, even if Mr. and Mrs. Jones had not been able to put in the extra $100 per month, this system would have dramatically reduced the time required to get them out from under all their debts.

Now that you've seen the comparison, which plan would you prefer to use for yourself and your family? Buried in debt for the rest of your life, or debt-free and financially healthy? It takes a plan and some discipline, but when you're able to start doing all the things you've always dreamed of, I believe you'll be happy you stuck with it.

Is the final payment usually a full payment when you are accelerating your payoff?

If not, what should you do with the difference?

Can you accelerate your payoff even if you don't have an Accelerator?

What does the Accelerator do?

Notes:

Enough about the Joneses! Let's talk about *you*!! It's time to work up your individual scenario. Let's start just like we did with the Joneses. First, fill out the Debt Information Sheet below. Make sure that you include *all* your debts.

Do not include utilities and other monthly *expenses;* just things that you *borrowed* for and that can be paid off. A good rule of thumb is – if you are paying interest, it's a debt. And unless you owe it to a close friend or family member, they're going to want interest in some form or another. (Occasionally, interest is built in so that it may not be noticed. If you have an obligation to pay something off, it's a debt.)

Also, make sure that you accurately list the *current* minimum monthly payment. It is important that you know the exact total of all your current minimum monthly payments. This is the starting number on which you will base your *Rapid-Debt-Payoff* program.

Make sure that this is a number you can live with every month. If you cannot pay this amount each month, adjustments will need to be made before you can implement this program successfully. (See the last part of this workbook if this is your situation.)

If you can't get an exact interest rate, principal balance, or payoff time, just get as close as you can; but fill in the blanks the best you are able to and we'll go from there. Please take the time to fill this out; this is a necessary step to start your program. (I have included two of the following sheets so you'll have a spare.)

Why is it important to know the exact total of all your current minimum monthly payments?

Notes:

Debt Information Sheet

Name_____ Date_____

Description of Debt	Min. Monthly Payment	Interest Rate	Principal Balance	Estimated Time to Payoff

Debt Information Sheet

Name_____ Date_____

Description of Debt	Min. Monthly Payment	Interest Rate	Principal Balance	Estimated Time to Payoff

Debt Priority Sheet

Now that you have filled out the Debt Information Sheet above and determined your accelerator in Step Three (even if this is zero), it's time to prioritize your debts. Using the formula that follows, fill out this sheet to determine your payoff order. If you don't remember how to do this, refer to the Jones example we did earlier.

Principal Bal. Due / (Min. Payment + Accelerator) = Priority Index

Description of Debt	Principal Balance	Minimum Payment	Accel- erator	Priority Index	Payoff Order

Debt Priority Sheet (cont.)

Description of Debt	Principal Balance	Minimum Payment	Accel- erator	Priority Index	Payoff Order

Debt Payoff Plan

Now that you have determined your payoff order, it's time to write down your payoff plan. List below all your debts in payoff order, and fill in the other blanks to complete your payoff plan. Refer back to the Jones example, if necessary. Remember to use the number from the **Total Payment** column as the **Accelerator** for the next line.

Order Number	Description of Debt	Starting Payment	Accel- erator	Total Payment	New Time to Payoff
1)		+	=		
2)		+	=		
3)		+	=		
4)		+	=		
5)		+	=		
6)		+	=		
7)		+	=		
8)		+	=		
9)		+	=		
10)		+	=		

Debt Payoff Plan (cont.)

Order Number	Description of Debt	Starting Payment		Accel-erator		Total Payment	New Time to Payoff
11)			+		=		
12)			+		=		
13)			+		=		
14)			+		=		
15)			+		=		
16)			+		=		
17)			+		=		
18)			+		=		
19)			+		=		
20)			+		=		

You may not be able to fill in the New Time to Payoff column with great accuracy. I would suggest using an estimate by dividing the principal amount due by the total amount you are paying, including your accelerator. You may have to add a little time to compensate for interest charges, but you can get a rough idea.

For example, if you have a debt of $2,000 that you will be paying $500 per month on, including your accelerator, you can figure 4 months; but add a little extra time due to interest charges. (It will still be only 5 months, with a partial last payment.)

Now that you have written out your Rapid-Debt-Payoff plan, I hope that you will stick with it and track your progress by writing down your payoff times each time one of your debts is paid in full. This should help keep you motivated to continue with your program.

I also suggest that every time you have a final payment that is less than the Total Payment on your Debt Payoff Plan sheet, that you take part of the difference, and reward yourself with a celebration dinner or something else you want. Apply the remainder of the difference, when such amount exists, to the next debt on your list. This will help you stay motivated and still get out of debt as quickly as possible.

If anything we've covered so far is unclear at this point, please review the previous material before going through the next section. The better your understanding of this information, the more likely you are to get the results you desire.

So far we've covered how the paying of compound interest over time can rob you of much needed dollars at retirement, and how to set up a plan to help you get out of debt as quickly as possible. And, I hope you are now convinced that, as far as compound interest goes (or investment yields in general), it is better to *receive* than it is to *give*!

If you will really utilize the steps that we've covered so far, get out of debt and stay out of debt, then the next section, **Step #5**, can help you to accumulate more money than you probably ever thought you could get your hands on. This is where the real payoff is for this program – *being able to live the way you've always wanted to – for the rest of your life.*

Approximately how long will it take for you to be completely debt-free?

Notes:

STEP #5

ACCUMULATING WEALTH

Now that you have learned the incredible difference between paying interest and receiving it, and have gotten completely out of debt – what now?

Well, let's return once again to the Jones example from earlier in this book. You can apply the concepts to your individual situation.

When we first met Mr. and Mrs. Jones, they were up to their eyeballs in debt and had no idea how, or even *why*, they should do anything about it.

First, we showed them the real-life effects of staying in debt, so they would know why a change was necessary. Then, we taught them how to set up a plan to get completely out of debt in a much shorter time than they otherwise would have been able to.

But that's not all there is to the *Trading Debt for Wealth* system. After getting rid of the debt, it's time to build wealth. This is the fun part! This is where it all pays off!

If we review the situation of Mr. and Mrs. Jones, we will remember that they were spending $2,700 per month servicing their debt. We can assume, for purposes of this example, that Mr. and Mrs. Jones can only afford to save the $100 per month from the example, for their retirement fund. Let's also assume that they save this amount in an account paying 6% per year (compounded monthly).

If Mr. and Mrs. Jones are both 30 years old when they start their savings program, here's how their accumulation will look between the ages of 30 and 65, when they plan to retire.

Age	Account Balance	Age	Account Balance
31	$ 1,234		
32	$ 2,543	45	$ 29,082
33	$ 3,934		
34	$ 5,410	50	$ 46,204
35	$ 6,977		
36	$ 8,641	55	$ 69,299
37	$ 10,407		
38	$ 12,283	60	$ 100,452
39	$ 14,274		
40	$ 16,388	65	$ 142,471

It is important to note that this example does not take into consideration any possible tax consequences. We have not yet dealt with taxation. We will do so shortly, to a limited extent.

So, how about that example? $142,471 seems like a pretty good amount of money to accumulate for only putting in $100 per month, right? Well, 35 years from now it won't seem like so much. And I assure you if Mr. and Mrs. Jones try to retire on that amount in 35 years, it won't seem like much.

Before we discuss how much more Mr. and Mrs. Jones might have using the *Trading Debt for Wealth* system, let's get an idea of how much they might need.

Let's assume that Mr. and Mrs. Jones believe they will need $2,000 per month in net income to retire on (in addition to their anticipated Social Security income), because their debts will be paid and the kids will be gone. This is, of course, stated in *today's dollars*. Thirty-five years from now, $2,000 per month will probably not buy much. We need to know how many *future dollars* will be needed to buy what $2,000 will buy today.

If we assume 4% inflation, in 35 years it will take almost $8,000 to buy what $2,000 can buy today. So how long will $142,000 last if you spend $8,000 per month? Not long enough.

I have several suggestions for this section, which can help solve your retirement income needs. Unfortunately, I can't list them all at once, and will have to address each one of them separately. When you know them all, you will be amazed at the difference that can be made in your account balance at retirement.

Rapid-Debt-Payoff

This is, of course, what we've been talking about throughout this workbook so far. Rapid-Debt-Payoff will make a huge difference when it comes to accumulating wealth for retirement.

Going back to the Jones example again, they had been paying $2,700 per month just to service their debt. This left them with only $100 to put towards their retirement (and $50 per month for their emergency fund). We re-routed that $100 per month for a total of $2,800 per month spent servicing debt. I said that I would show you how we will make up for this later. Well, now it's later.

By following the *Trading Debt for Wealth* method, Mr. and Mrs. Jones paid off all their debts in approximately six years. No, they didn't save that $100 per month from age 30 to age 36. But at age 36, instead of only being able to save $100 per month, now the Joneses can save $2,800 per month – because they have no debts!

Let's see how their accumulation looks now. We will not start at age 30 because they spent the first six years just paying off debts, without accumulating anything for retirement. We will start them at age 36 and show their first accumulation year at age 37. (We will use the same 6% interest as before, but now at a savings rate of $2,800 per month.)

Age	Account Balance	Age	Account Balance
31	$ 0		
32	$ 0	45	$ 399,672
33	$ 0		
34	$ 0	50	$ 734,453
35	$ 0		
36	$ 0	55	$ 1,186,024
37	$ 34,540		
38	$ 71,209	60	$ 1,795,124
39	$ 110,141		
40	$ 151,474	65	$ 2,616,710

Again, this does not include any allowance for taxes. (This will be addressed later.) I think you can see how this compares to the previous example of the Joneses putting away that $100 per month, and continuing to pay on their debts for years and years. This one difference alone, not considering any of the other investment suggestions to follow, made a long-term difference of well over $2,000,000!

How does the second example accumulate over $2,000,000 more than the first example?

Accumulation Time

Accumulation time is a very important factor in determining how much money you will have at retirement. There may or may not be anything you can do about this, depending upon your circumstances. But it is important to make the best of your individual situation.

If you are now age 55 or 60 and have substantial debt to pay off before you can start an aggressive accumulation program, don't expect to have nearly as much to retire on as you would if you had started 10 or 20 years earlier. However, please don't get discouraged and think that you might as well not try. It is even more important that you get serious about this quickly.

Even though the results may not be as incredible as they could have been had you started at an earlier age, there may still be a lot that can be done for you. If you are very close to retirement age right now, you should probably see a competent professional and have a custom plan written for your individual situation. You can learn the important concepts taught in this workbook, but it is also important to consult a professional.

Here are some things to consider if you are older and don't feel that you have enough time to accumulate adequate retirement funds:

- Do you have a source of income that may allow you to leave retirement funds to accumulate for some length of time after your chosen retirement date?

- How would you feel about working beyond the date you had planned to retire?

- How about a part-time job or business after retirement? Do you have a hobby or other interest that you would enjoy doing in your spare time, which could also be used as a means of income?

- Repositioning assets to increase income should be done with the assistance of a competent professional, who will put *your* best interest before his or her own.

If you are younger and have plenty of time before retirement, don't put off planning for your future. If you look at either of the above two examples, you will see the dramatic difference in account balance that occurs in the last five to ten years of accumulation. It may seem that your efforts in your earlier years won't make much difference, but please remember this:

If you postpone planning for the accumulation of your retirement funds, it's not the smaller "first-dollars-invested" that you will lose –

it's the much larger, "last-dollars-accumulated" that you will give up. In many cases, this will exceed $1,000,000.

Rate of Return

When we say "interest rate" as it applies to your investments or savings, we really mean Return on Investment (ROI) in general. When you invest in *equities,* such as stocks and stock mutual funds, then you're not really receiving *interest*. You are receiving *dividends* and *capital gains*, which add up to an overall rate of return on your investment.

When you invest in *debt* (not to be confused with *going into debt*), then you are actually receiving *interest*. Examples of debt investments are savings accounts, certificates of deposit, bonds, and U.S. Government securities. (Some debt instruments may also offer opportunities to receive capital gains; but this is not addressed in this book.)

The rate of return that you receive on your investments can have a profound effect on your account balance, over the long run. The choice of an investment vehicle for every situation cannot possibly be defined here. But there are some points to be made here which can be of great help to you when you are trying to decide which investments are right for you.

Before we say any more about specific types of investments, it is important that you get a feel for how much differences in interest rates, or *rates of return*, can impact your account balance in the long run.

In keeping with my attempt to bring you easy ways to figure things out without having to use a financial calculator, here's an easy formula you can use to estimate how much you can accumulate over a specific period of time, at different interest rates. This formula is called **The Rule of 72.**

72 / interest rate = number of years to double your money.

The Rule of 72 simply states that the number 72 divided by any given interest rate, will give you the approximate number of years it will take to double your money at that given rate. For example, if your rate of return were 6%, it would take approximately 12 years to double your money. If the rate of return were 12%, it would take approximately 6 years to double your money. I didn't make this one up, so I don't know why it works – it just works.

Let's look at a comparison of interest rates using the Rule of 72. Let's compare 6% to 12%, and see just how big of a difference the interest rate on your investment can really make to your account balance in the long run.

For this example, let's assume that at age 30, you made a one-time investment of $2,000 at a 6% rate of return. (Again, tax consequences will not be considered here.) 72 divided by 6 equals 12. So your money will double approximately every 12 years.

Age	Account Balance
30	$2,000
42	$4,000
54	$8,000
66	$16,000

As you can see, your money will double every 12 years, growing from the $2,000 you originally invested, into $16,000 over a 36 year period.

I have asked numerous people what they think would happen, in this example, if we were to double the interest rate, but leave everything else the same. Many have said they believe that the ending account balance would also double. This sounds like a reasonable conclusion, doesn't it? What do you think will happen if we double the interest rate?

Before trying to figure this out mathematically, take your best guess at what the result would be if you doubled the interest rate in the above example.

Now try to get the answer using the **Rule of 72**.

Notes:

Here's the example again, only this time at 6% and at 12%, side by side:

Age	Balance at 6%	Balance at 12%
30	$2,000	$2,000
36		$4,000
42	$4,000	$8,000
48		$16,000
54	$8,000	$32,000
60		$64,000
66	$16,000	$128,000

All we did is double the rate of return. That's all. And look at the results over the 36-year period. At 6%, the bottom line is $16,000. At 12%, the bottom line is $128,000! This is many times more than the 6% result, not just twice. The rate of return over a long period of time can make a huge difference in your bottom line.

Can you see how all these factors working together could make an incredible difference in your standard of living at retirement? So far, we've gone over these three factors:

1) **Rapid-Debt-Payoff** – This gives you a lot more money to invest.

2) **Accumulation Period** – The last few years of a long-term plan may earn more than all the other years combined.

3) **Rate of Return** – Combined with a long accumulation period, getting higher rates of return can multiply your account balance many times.

There are more things that can make a big difference in your account balance in the long run; but I wanted you to see how these three can work together before moving on.

Can you see how making the best of the three factors above would give you a lot more money in the long run?

_____

How can you use all three to your advantage?

_____

Make up your own example using the Rule of 72 and compare any two interest rates below. Start with your present age.

Risk vs. Reward

If you are surprised at the huge difference that a higher rate of return can make over a long period of time, you are probably also wondering where to get those higher rates of return.

It is important to know a few things before rushing out and jumping into anything that may offer a high rate of return. The first thing to know is that this catchy phrase that everyone has heard for years is not exactly correct:

The higher the risk, the higher the return.

This statement is not necessarily true. There are many risky ventures that would probably lose all your money if you invested in them. Actually, the above phrase is almost true; it's just wrong enough to be dangerous. Some people think that this means they can put their money into something risky, and because it's risky, this means they *will* receive a high return.

Generally speaking (but not always), if you want to receive a higher rate of return, you will have to accept greater risk of losing your principal. This does not mean that if you accept more risk, you will get a higher return; you might lose all your money. It just means that most investments will only pay higher rates of return to compensate the investor for accepting a higher degree of risk.

There are some situations that may offer a high degree of risk, without the opportunity to earn as high a return as should be offered, considering the risk. You need to compare opportunities and take the best one for the degree of risk that you are willing to accept.

Another thing to realize is that there is more than one type of risk. If you are so conservative with your investments that you only invest in securities guaranteed by the United States government, you will be subjecting yourself to *purchasing power risk.* Because of the low rates of return, your money may not keep its value after inflation, and won't buy as much as you will need it to when you retire.

The fact is, you can choose investments that will offer you high rates of return over time. You just need to know when it's appropriate for you, and beware of the risks involved.

Let's say that you are keeping your money in a savings account at your local bank, and after seeing the illustration of the Rule of 72, you decide you'd like to end up having a lot more money than the bank is going to give you. What do you do? Well, this depends on a few factors, such as:

1) How long do you intend to leave this money alone before using it?

2) If an emergency came up, would you need this money to be instantly accessible, or do you have other funds set aside for emergencies?

3) Would you get stressed out if the value of your account were to go down for a while? How would you deal with the fluctuations?

4) What is your age? If you were to lose money, do you have time to make more?

Generally speaking, more *aggressive* investments, those offering higher potential returns in exchange for your willingness to accept a higher degree of risk, are a good idea if you are young enough to sit back and relax through the ups and downs of the market. These are generally *equities*, and fluctuate in value over time.

The advantage that equity investments have over debt investments is, over the long term, that they tend to pay significantly higher rates of return. And you saw the long-term effects of obtaining a significantly higher rate of return.

When investment professionals talk about how risky a specific investment is, what they usually measure to determine this, is *volatility*, the fluctuations in the value of the investment. And just because an investment fluctuates in value over time, does not mean that it is a bad investment.

If you invest in a good stock, for example, the value of the stock will go up, and it will go down. But over a period of time, a good stock is likely to earn a considerably higher return for you than most debt instruments will. When it comes to volatility, the key is how long you are able to leave your investments alone.

Generally, the less-risky, more *liquid* types of investments (those that allow you to access your money quickly, without loss of principal) will pay a lower rate of return over time, and are good for saving money over a shorter time period. It's a good idea to be able to leave your money in "the market" for at least several years if you want to invest in equities.

As you get very close to retirement age, you will want to think about reducing the risk of loss of your principal. Hopefully by now, you will have built up a nice-sized nest egg, and won't need as high an interest rate to accumulate sufficient wealth to retire comfortably.

The idea here is that when you have plenty of time before retirement, if the value of your investments have gone down, there is still time for the value to go back up before you retire. If you are retired, or are very close to retirement, there may not be that much time.

Hopefully, by the time you retire, you will have enough money saved up to live comfortably on a lower rate of return. That way, if the stock market goes down, your income doesn't get slashed, adding financial stress to your life when you should be enjoying yourself.

During your ***accumulation stage*** (that time in your life when you are not living off your investments, but rather, contributing to them), you will probably need to take on a reasonable degree of risk in order to get the rate of return you need to build up a large estate. That way you won't need a high rate of return when you retire. If you have enough money, you can retire very comfortably on a lower rate of return, making sure that you won't lose the money you are now relying on to live.

Of course, the object is not to go looking for risk; it's to find the highest quality investments possible, within the risk category that is appropriate for your temperament, goals, and stage of life (*time horizon*). Then, should you decide to invest, try to minimize the risk as much as possible. One very popular way of accomplishing this is to invest in ***mutual funds***.

Why do some investments offer higher *potential* returns than others?

Should you look for "risky" investments if you may need quick access to your money?

Why or why not?

Mutual Funds

People used to ask me all the time what a mutual fund is. Or they would ask me how a mutual fund compares with some other kind of investment. A mutual fund isn't actually an investment, in and of itself. Basically, a mutual fund is a bunch of people putting their money into a big pot. That pot then invests the money, and the people who have their money in the pot own *shares* in the pot, or mutual fund.

Mutual funds can help solve two issues related to risk:

1) Professional Management

2) Diversification

Professional Management: Let's say you want to invest in the stock market. You don't know the first thing about investing in stocks, but you know you want a high rate of return. A mutual fund has a professional fund manager who makes the investment decisions. You only have to decide which fund(s) to invest in.

Diversification: One way people reduce their risk is to diversify their holdings. If you were to put all your money in one stock, and the company you invested in went out of business, you'd be in trouble.

But, if you bought ten stocks instead of one, your loss from the one that went out of business could be offset by the success of other companies that did very well. This is diversification – not putting all your eggs in one basket.

Diversification is primarily a method of reducing risk, while still keeping your money where the overall result can be a high rate of return. So how about your more conservative investments?

Usually, the higher the risk, the more important it is to diversify. Many people just think they need to diversify, period. They don't understand the reasoning behind diversification. If the purpose of diversification is to reduce risk, do you need to diversify your guaranteed or extremely conservative investments?

Well, there may be more than one reason to not have all your eggs in one basket. You may need staggered maturities, or have other reasons to diversify, but the risk reason may be pretty much eliminated. If you have $100,000 invested in securities guaranteed by the U.S. Government, you don't need to split it up into $10,000 chunks to feel your money is safe. It's guaranteed either way.

Mutual funds can be used to invest in a wide variety of financial instruments. One mutual fund may specialize in aggressive growth (stocks of smaller companies, which reinvest a large percentage of their earnings to grow and expand quickly). Another may specialize in blue-chip stocks (larger, well-established companies that pay a reliable dividend), corporate bonds, municipal bonds, government securities, commodities futures, specific industries, specific areas of the world, etc., etc., etc.

Other funds may be *balanced*, including a variety of different types of investments for different objectives. There are literally thousands of funds to choose from, so the possibilities may seem endless. It may be appropriate for you to invest in several different types of funds. It all depends upon your situation.

If you would like to save money on your investments, you can chose to invest exclusively in *no-load* mutual funds. A *loaded* fund can take up to 8.5% of each deposit you make, to pay the sales commission. No-load funds generally perform as well, and there's no commission. You will need to be able to make your own investment decisions, however, as a salesperson will not come help you for free.

We could pursue this topic is much greater detail, but that is not the purpose of this workbook. If you are interested in learning more about mutual funds, there are numerous books and articles written on the subject, not to mention all the financial salespeople who are anxious to help you. Your local bookstore or magazine rack is a great place to start.

How can investing in mutual funds help to reduce risk?

NOTES:

Dollar Cost Averaging

Though I do not want to write another 500 pages about investing in mutual funds, I do want to discuss one specific strategy that applies to them. This technique can be used with other types of investments as well; however, sometimes it's not practical due to the high dollar amounts that could be required, and other factors not necessary for our discussion.

For a long-term mutual fund investor, like many of you will be when saving for retirement, dollar cost averaging can be an excellent strategy to apply. Not only is this technique easy and convenient to use, but it can also increase your overall rate of return, without increasing your risk. Sounds good, doesn't it?

Here's how dollar cost averaging works. Let's suppose that you want to accumulate shares of ABC Mutual Fund as a savings vehicle for your retirement. Let's assume that this fund is currently selling at $10 per share. Because you have paid off all of your debts (using this wonderful program, of course), you can afford to save $1,000 per month for your retirement.

That means that you can afford to buy 100 shares per month, at the current price. If you did this, _your_ **average cost per share** would be the same as _the fund's_ **average price per share**, (for the days you invested). Here, I'll show you:

Date	ABC Fund Price	Number of Shares You Bought	Amount of Your Investment
Jan 15	$10.00	100	$1,000.00
Feb 15	$12.50	100	$1,250.00
Mar 15	$14.75	100	$1,475.00
Apr 15	$11.25	100	$1,125.00
May 15	$9.60	100	$960.00
Jun 15	$8.10	100	$810.00
Jul 15	$7.15	100	$715.00
Aug 15	$6.95	100	$695.00
Sep 15	$7.85	100	$785.00
Oct 15	$9.85	100	$985.00
Nov 15	$13.35	100	$1,335.00
Dec 15	$16.00	100	$1,600.00

To calculate the average price per share, you simply add up all the prices in the column, and divide by the number of prices you added up. The total of the amounts in the **ABC Fund Price** column is $127.35. Dividing this number by 12, the total number of entries, gives us $10.61 as the fund's *average price per share*. Since you bought the same number of shares each month, your *average cost per share* will also be $10.61.

If you change the number of shares that you buy each month, your average cost per share will be different than the fund's average price per share. Let me show you what I mean. This time, instead of purchasing the same *number of shares* per month, you will invest the *same dollar amount* each month.

Date	ABC Fund Price	Number of Shares You Bought	Amount of Your Investment
Jan 15	$10.00	100.00	$1,000.00
Feb 15	$12.50	80.00	$1,000.00
Mar 15	$14.75	67.80	$1,000.00
Apr 15	$11.25	88.89	$1,000.00
May 15	$9.60	104.17	$1,000.00
Jun 15	$8.10	123.46	$1,000.00
Jul 15	$7.15	139.86	$1,000.00
Aug 15	$6.95	143.88	$1,000.00
Sep 15	$7.85	127.39	$1,000.00
Oct 15	$9.85	101.52	$1,000.00
Nov 15	$13.35	74.91	$1,000.00
Dec 15	$16.00	62.50	$1,000.00

Comparing the two examples above, we notice a few things. In the first example, your monthly investment fluctuated widely, which could be very inconvenient for your monthly budget, if it's even possible. The second example leaves your monthly investment exactly the same every month.

In the first example, you purchased the same number of shares each month, causing your average cost per share to be the same as the fund's average price per share. Now, that's a lot better than having your average cost per share be more than the fund's average price per share. But, what if your average cost per share could be less than the fund's average price per share, simply by leaving your monthly investment amount exactly the same every month, and allowing the number of shares purchased to fluctuate?

Let's see what happens when we calculate your average cost per share in the second example, and compare it to the fund's average price per share for the same days. If we add up the total number of shares you purchased during the 12-month period above, we get 1,214.38 shares. Adding up the $1,000 per month you invested multiplied by the 12 months, we get $12,000. Watch this:

Total Cost / Total # of Shares = Average Cost per Share

$12,000 divided by 1,214.38 shares = $9.88 per share.

Remember that in the first of the two examples above, your average cost per share was $10.61. In the second example, your average cost per share is $9.88. This can be a significant difference in the long run, and can put more money in your pocket, while at the same time being the most convenient way to invest over the long term.

How did this happen? The two examples use exactly the same dates and share prices. If you look at the first example, you will notice that you are buying the same number of shares regardless of the price. In the second example, however, you will notice that *if the price goes up, you bought fewer shares. If the price goes down, you bought more shares.*

When you compare, you have purchased fewer shares at a high price, and more shares at a low price. *You bought more shares at a below average price than you did at an above average price.* This is how you get an average cost per share that is lower than the fund's average price per share, creating an extra profit above what the fund actually pays.

The easiest way to do this is to choose a monthly amount you can commit to, and sign up for a monthly bank draft to invest in the mutual fund of your choice. If you can leave your money in the mutual fund for a fairly long period of time, you can invest in an aggressive fund. The value will go up and down, but over the long run these funds can offer very high rates of return, and be even higher using *Dollar Cost Averaging.*

Explain how *dollar cost averaging* can increase your rate of return:

Tax Deferral

Finally we address the topic of **Income Tax.** One of the most feared and dreaded subjects since the dawn of time, taxation affects just about everything we touch. The focus of this brief discussion will be on how income tax can affect our investments, and what we can do about it.

If we invest our hard-earned money over a long period of time, using all the wonderful ideas we can come up with, but we disregard the effects of taxation, we will be letting a lot of money slip through our fingers, some of it unnecessarily.

Let's do yet another example. I'm using a financial calculator for this, so you don't need to work this out for yourself, just follow along.

Let's assume that you want to save $400 per month for 35 years at 12% rate of return. At the end of your 35 years, you should have more than $2.5 million. But that's before Uncle Sam takes his share. If you are in the 28% tax bracket, your 12% rate of return will become an *after-tax* return of 8.64% (12% less the 28% tax). This results in a bottom line of a little over $1 million. Uncle Sam will happily relieve you of over half of your money. (Your *Marginal Tax Bracket* is the rate of tax you pay on the last dollar you earn.)

This example is only referring to the tax due on what your dollars earn every year. The effects can reach much farther than this, however. Let's assume that the $400 per month that you want to save is *taxable income* (as most income is). After paying 28% Federal Income Tax, you are left only $288 of your $400 to invest each month.

What started out as $400 per month to invest at 12%, thanks to taxation, is now $288 per month at 8.64%. This means that instead of winding up with $2,572,384, you will only have $774,069, due to federal income tax. This may still sound like a lot, but the point is – taxes have taken most of your money! Without taxes, you'd have over $2.5 million. After taxes, you have less than $800,000.

There are two ways that income taxation can reduce the amount of money you accumulate (not to mention the effects of Estate Taxation, which is beyond the scope of this book). The first way is by reducing the amount you can take from your paycheck to invest. The second way is by taxing you every year you receive interest income or gains on the money you invest.

There are certain things that the IRS will allow us to do, that can make a big difference in the amount of money we will get to keep instead of paying in taxes. Here are a few.

Qualified Retirement Accounts

There are many different types of *qualified plans*. Each different type of organization seems to have something different that the IRS will allow for its employees. There are far too many details to include in this book, but the idea is the same. Every dollar that you put into your qualified retirement plan will reduce your taxable income by that amount. This does not include the Social Security or Medicare tax, but if you are in the 28% tax bracket, the $288 you might be able to afford to invest after paying tax on your income, instantly becomes $400 if you invest it *"pre-tax"*.

In addition, after putting all those *pre-tax dollars* to work for you, *all* your money will stay in your account, earning interest year after year, until you pull it out. There is a catch, of course. These taxes are not eliminated completely, but just deferred until you take out your money. (There are also penalties for early withdrawal and other details to be aware of – see your investment advisor.)

This is not an even trade off. The amount of money that you can accumulate by having *all* your money working for you for all those years, instead of only the amount that would be left over after taxation, is much, much more that the after-tax alternative. Even after you pay your taxes way down the road, you'll have a lot more left over to use however you like.

The 401(k) Matching Plan

Generally speaking, it is a good idea to use all the money you can get your hands on to first get out from under all your debts, then finish accumulating your emergency fund, and finally, to save for retirement. Other savings goals can be inserted as needed.

However, there is an exception to this rule that needs to be mentioned. When your employer is willing to match your contributions to a 401(k) or other retirement plan, I would strongly suggest that you not turn down this free money.

Try to find a way to still have an adequate accelerator while making the maximum contribution that your employer will match. I do not suggest making a higher contribution than your employer will match, until you are out of debt. But if it's at all possible, don't turn down this free money.

Are you better off paying taxes on investment income now, or after it has accumulated over a long period of time? Why?

Individual Retirement Accounts (IRAs)

An Individual Retirement Account can offer you an opportunity to invest your retirement money in a tax-advantaged account, independent of your employment. Your money will grow tax-deferred until retirement. You may or may not qualify to have the amount of your annual contribution subtracted from your taxable income, but account earnings are tax-deferred either way.

The rules for IRAs continue to change over time. In 2012, annual contributions to an IRA still cannot exceed $5,000 (or your earnings, if less than $5,000). If you are age 50 by the end of 2012 your contribution limit is $6,000 per year (or your earnings, if less than $6,000). Spouses are required to have separate accounts, and now each spouse can contribute $5,000 ($6,000 if age 50+), even if one is a full-time homemaker.

If you are Married Filing Jointly, your full contribution is deductable as long as your Modified Adjusted Gross Income (MAGI, or Modified AGI) does not exceed $91,000. For incomes between $91,000 and $111,000 your deductibility is phased out, and if your MAGI is above $111,000 your contributions are non-tax deductable.

If you are single, your deductions are 100% deductable up to $57,000 MAGI and phase out between $57,000 and $67,000 MAGI. If there's no retirement plan at work, these limits are higher – see your investment professional for more details.

Most of the common investment vehicles are now approved for IRAs. In other words, you can choose a mutual fund or stock or other type of investment, and put it in your IRA account so you get the tax advantages. An IRA is a type of account, not a type of investment.

There are still some restrictions on types of investments, and there is much more to know about IRAs than we've gone over here. This is such a good way to invest, that I would highly recommend learning more about IRAs, and using one as part of your wealth-building retirement strategy.

The IRA we've been talking about so far is a ***Traditional IRA***. There are now other types of IRAs as well.

Roth IRA

The Taxpayer Relief Act of 1997 created the ***Roth IRA***. Your contributions to a Roth IRA are *nondeductible*. Your contribution will not reduce the amount of income on which you pay tax.

However, the Roth IRA has a very attractive quality to it. Your distributions are not just tax-deferred, they're *tax-free!* Not only do you get the benefit of having all your money working for you, without it being taxed every year; but, when you go to take it out – you pay no taxes! This can be a huge benefit. After building up a few million dollars for your retirement, it can save you a fortune if you don't have to pay taxes on any of the distributions.

Like the regular IRA, annual contributions are limited to $5,000 per person. Unlike the regular IRA, you aren't required to start taking distributions at age 70 ½. With a Roth IRA, the $5,000 annual contribution limit is phased out (reduced to zero contribution allowed) for individual filers with Modified AGIs between $105,000 and $120,000. For Married Filing Jointly, the limit is phased out for Modified AGIs of between $167,000 and $177,000.

There are more details that you will want to become familiar with, in order to fully understand the Roth IRA; but I would strongly urge you to check this out. Living tax-free at retirement can be an incredible advantage you won't want to miss out on.

SIMPLE IRA

A SIMPLE Plan is a type of IRA or tax-favored retirement plan that certain small employers and self-employed people can set up to benefit their employees, including themselves. If you are eligible, you may reduce your compensation by a certain percentage each pay period and have this *salary reduction contribution* made on your behalf.

The employer must make either matching contributions or nonelective contributions equaling 2% of your compensation. The overall limit on contributions to SIMPLE IRAs is higher than Traditional or Roth IRAs. See a financial professional for more help with this type of account. If you're a self-employed business owner, also ask about a SEP IRA.

How do Roth IRAs and SIMPLE IRAs differ from other tax-deferred plans?

Variable Universal Life (VUL)

Variable Universal Life is a type of life insurance. I will describe this briefly, but will not go into all the details, as life insurance is not the topic of this workbook.

Variable Universal Life Insurance is one way that many people have found to help them accumulate tax-deferred savings for retirement. The advantage of VUL is that, because this is a life insurance product, tax laws offer special advantages.

If you buy a VUL policy, the cash value part of your policy can grow tax-deferred. And you can choose from a variety of mutual funds to have that cash value invested in. In other words, you can still be invested in mutual funds, but have the tax deferral element of a life insurance policy.

Another advantage of VUL is that you can "borrow" the cash value out of your policy, in many cases, *interest-free!* In many policies (the one's I would consider), the interest rate they charge you for borrowing the cash value out of your policy, is the same rate that they pay you for having the money in the policy. These two rates cancel each other out, and you are basically using the money interest-free.

Why would you want to do this? Because borrowed money is not taxable income. You never have to pay income taxes on the money you "borrow". So if your method of "withdrawing" the money out of your policy is to borrow it out, you'll get it tax-free. Yes, the IRS knows all about this and it's perfectly legal.

There are also disadvantages to VUL. It can be expensive. There may be surrender charges, monthly or annual fees, and other details to watch for. For example, if you are older, the *cost of insurance* part of your premium can become so expensive that it may eat into, and eventually, completely use up your cash value – unless you pay enough into the policy to prevent that from happening.

You also need to be aware of how much insurance you need. This book does not cover this subject, but a VUL policy may be too expensive to be the only thing protecting your family against the loss of your income. If you chose VUL, you may need to supplement your coverage with a less-expensive *term insurance* policy.

Term Insurance is temporary insurance with no cash value. It is designed to protect you for a finite period of time such as 1, 5, 10, or 20 years. It is usually the appropriate choice for temporary needs. For example, the support of your children until they are of age could easily be covered by a 20-year term policy. (By the time the policy expires, the kids are grown and hopefully don't rely on you for their support.)

Without delving too deeply into the area of *Insurance Planning*, it is generally a good idea to use "temporary insurance" (term) while you are young and in the Rapid-Debt-Payoff phase of life. You can usually obtain adequate coverage to protect your family from the loss of your income, without paying a horrendous premium. The money you save every month on premiums can be used as your *Accelerator*, and greatly reduce your debt payoff time. Then, you will have more years to invest aggressively for your future.

As far as a VUL policy goes, I would probably go for the Roth (or SIMPLE) IRA first, but if all your debts are paid off and you have money left over after maxing out your IRA, a VUL policy may be worth looking into. Make sure that you see a competent and trustworthy professional before you decide if this option is right for you.

Commission-Free Insurance

Saving money on your life insurance premiums, as long as you maintain the appropriate coverage, is one way to help you "find your Accelerator". It will also increase the amount you are able to invest for your future.

If you are older, or you need a large amount of life insurance coverage, you will notice that your premiums are rather high. A large percentage of your life insurance premium may be due to the commission paid to the salesperson.

Most people are not aware that it is possible to buy life insurance without paying a commission. A former associate of mine is an expert in this field, and I have seen him save his clients up to $45,000 per year on their life insurance premiums!

With a special license, he is able to obtain insurance for his clients that is far less expensive than usual, because the policy does not pay a commission to a salesperson. Instead, he charges a fee for his time. This enables him to give the best possible insurance advice without having any incentive to sell a policy to earn a commission.

If your insurance needs are quite inexpensive, it may actually be less costly to buy from a commissioned salesperson, because the fee can be significant. However, if your premiums are high, paying the professional fee can save an incredible amount of money, if it reduces your premiums by thousands per year.

If you think this situation may apply to you, look into Commission-Free Insurance, or the services of an LIC, or *Licensed Insurance Counselor*. Availability of this option and the title of the professional consultant may vary from state to state. This information is valid in my home state of Texas.

NOTES:

What About My Mortgage?

You will notice that the *Trading Debt for Wealth* plan is designed to get your mortgage paid off quickly, as well as your other debts. Why should you pay off your house instead of taking advantage of what is often referred to as "the only good tax write-off we have left"?

First of all, if you plan on selling your home in the near future, you don't need to worry about paying it off early. That debt will be paid when you sell the home. (Though I should point out that pre-paying principal will still reduce the interest you'll pay and give you more equity to walk away with when you do sell, so this can be a very good idea.) But for the home you plan on staying in a long time, I suggest rapid payoff. There are several reasons for this:

(1) Having your home paid for will significantly increase the amount of income that you can invest for your retirement. It usually only takes a few years to pay it off with this method, then all that money you were using for mortgage payments can be invested. The difference in your retirement fund can be substantial.

(2) Having absolutely no debt will put you in a position of financial strength, should something happen unexpectedly to reduce your income or increase your expenses, such as medical bills for a serious illness in the family.

(3) The rate of return on your money is really pretty good, considering it's guaranteed. Investments that are guaranteed pay low rates of return, because there is no *risk premium*. If you look at your mortgage rate, it is probably higher than you would be able to get putting your money into a CD.

(4) If your mortgage amount is $100,000 at 8% for 30 years, you will pay more than $264,000 in payments for your home. If you were to pay your home off in 7 years instead of 30 years, your total payments would be approximately $130,000. This is a savings of approximately $134,000, not to mention the interest you are earning by continuing to make those house payments—into your retirement fund!

(5) The tax write-off benefit of paying on a mortgage may not be as attractive as you think. If you are in the 28% marginal tax bracket, it is true that you will save $28 in taxes for every $100 you pay in qualified mortgage interest, as long as you are still in the 28% bracket after deductions.

However, in order to really get a $28 benefit for each $100 you spend in qualified mortgage interest, you must have other itemized deductions at least equal to your standard-deduction amount. If you are *married filing jointly*, you will now have a standard deduction of $11,900 – even if you don't have any write-offs. You can itemize *or* take the standard deduction; you don't get both.

For example, if your total itemized deductions (Married Filing Jointly, 28% tax bracket) were $12,000, you saved a whopping $28 in addition to what you would have paid using the standard deduction of $11,900. That certainly doesn't make it worth paying all that interest, does it?

In short, the interest rate on your home may not be high, and there may be some tax incentive to keeping a mortgage. But, when you look at all the factors, including being less vulnerable to adverse changes in your personal financial situation, and having more money to invest after saving all that interest, including your home in your Rapid-Debt-Payoff program is a wise decision in many cases. Living totally debt-free has advantages that go far beyond comparing interest rates or tax incentives.

List 3 good reasons to pay off your mortgage early:

(1)

(2)

(3)

Maximizing Your Returns

There are a variety of ways people attempt to maximize their investment returns. A few ideas will be listed here. After determining how much risk you are willing to take, what you want to do is maximize your return, within that level of risk. Here's an example:

Certificates of Deposit

If you go to your bank and ask for a CD, they will be happy to tell you what types, maturities, and interest rates they offer.

But, CD rates vary across the United States. Instead of going to your local bank, you can have a *CD Broker* get you a CD from whoever happens to be paying the highest rate of interest at the time. They're still federally insured, so your risk has not been increased, just your return.

Real Estate

I like real estate investing. It's not foolproof, but there is a lot of potential there, and if you really learn how to do it the rewards can be great. This is not a book about real estate investing, but that is the subject of one of my other books, *The Rico Strategy®*, available at Amazon.com, bookstores and other online retailers.

Many people think that you can't lose money investing in real estate – that is not correct. You can lose your shirt. But it is something that you can get good at that can provide superior returns to you if you take the time to learn it well and invest in your own abilities instead of investing in the financial markets.

Small Business

The same thing applies here. The financial markets are designed to allow people to use financial resources when they choose to use them. Those who allow their money to be used are compensated for allowing their money to be used. Those wanting to use money that does not belong to them compensate those who allow their money to be used.

In addition to a time premium, those who allow their money to be used in riskier endeavors are paid a *risk premium*. But remember that accepting risk means that you may never see your money again, not to mention your risk premium. The financial markets are efficient and are not designed to compensate you for more than you provide – use of your money, along with a risk premium.

The way to actually create wealth is to invest in real assets. That would be real estate or an asset that allows you to produce and sell a product for a profit. If you engage in a business activity, depending on the activity and your level of expertise, you may earn returns generously in excess of what you can earn in the financial markets, accepting similar risk.

Of course, if you can actually learn to outperform others in the financial markets, you can earn superior returns. But remember that you're competing with educated financial professionals who devote their entire lives to winning at that game.

You may be better off simply learning these strategies of how to best deal with the money you make, earn compound interest as opposed to paying it, and invest your money in such a way that the amounts you are setting aside are growing without accepting too much risk.

If you want to earn returns that greatly exceed the normal returns in the financial markets, I believe engaging in a business activity or shrewd real estate investing is the way to accomplish that. Of course, stay diversified. If you start early and stick to a plan, you can afford the luxury of concerning yourself more with the return *of* your investment than the return *on* your investment.

List 2 ways to improve your rates of return without accepting too much risk:

1)

2)

Notes:

Notes:

STEP #6

SETTING AND ACHIEVING GOALS

This is an important section, though it will be brief. I will not attempt to take the place of the stacks of books written on how to achieve your goals (including my new book, *Success for Losers*, available everywhere). But I will include a few suggestions here that may prove useful to you.

There is a reason why this section is listed as the last step instead of the first step of this program. Usually, setting your goals would be the first step of anything you want to achieve. But in this case, you may not have any idea as to what goals you should set until you have gone through the program and discovered what the possibilities are.

Now that you have gone through the program, and have an idea about how long it will take you to become completely debt-free, you can set a goal to achieve this result. Obstacles may appear – things you never thought of, that will try to prevent you from achieving your goals. This happens. That's why it is important to have a pre-planned strategy to achieve your goals, even if it becomes difficult.

Here are some ideas that you should keep in mind. These things can really make a difference during the times of adversity or lack of motivation:

(1) Decide on a specific goal, and *write it down.* A goal that is not written down is only a wish. Be serious about this. Put this written goal someplace you can see it every day. Make sure your goal is realistic, based on what you have learned in this program.

(2) State your goal in the present tense, with an exact date, and add a positive emotion. Your brain will respond better this way, using your subconscious mind to help your actions become more compatible with the achievement of your goal. Here's an example:

As of July 1st, 2019, I am completely debt-free, and loving it!!

Here's another example, to use after you become debt-free:

I enjoy contributing $2,500 into my retirement account each month!

You get the idea. If you make this goal sound exciting and fun, it will be more motivating. The exact date will help you close in on your goal. Never use time frames like "In five years, I will be out of debt." Five years never comes because it's always five years away. If it's a goal with a deadline, use the exact date.

(3) Set short-term goals, also. These seem more realistic. If your first accelerated debt can be paid off in 6 months, great! Write it down. There is room on your 3x5 goal-card for two goals, a long-term goal and a short-term goal.

(4) Reward yourself when you achieve a goal. This keeps you motivated to continue reaching other goals. Determine your reward in advance and write it down. Make sure your rewards are motivating but not excessive. Remember the purpose of your goals is to get out of debt and build wealth.

Each time you pay off another debt, there may be money left over due to a partial last payment. You may decide to use some of that money to take your spouse out for a nice dinner; or you may prefer to buy something that you will enjoy and that will help keep you motivated to continue setting and reaching financial goals.

(5) Do *not* go into debt for a reward. Abandon those counterproductive habits and replace them with productive ones, like self-discipline.

(6) Each time a credit card is paid off, make a big deal about cutting it up. I would suggest, if you are married, that you cut it up together as you are about to buy, eat, or enjoy your chosen reward.

(7) Have an emergency fund and an account for non-monthly expenses, so you are not tempted or forced to temporarily stop your Rapid-Debt-Payoff program any more than absolutely necessary.

As I mentioned earlier in this program, it is okay to use your monthly Accelerator as a source of emergency cash until you have an adequate fund built up, because that is preferable to postponing starting your Rapid-Debt-Payoff program for the several years it would take to save it up.

However, I still recommend contributing a small amount each month to an emergency fund so that there is always something there, in case you have an emergency immediately after sending in your monthly *accelerator* money to pay off a debt. I also recommend having a separate account set up for non-monthly expenses. This way, it is unlikely that many surprises will come along and knock you off track.

(8) For the big goal, get a big reward. This suggestion is for those whose financial situation does not prohibit this idea, due to needing to retire soon or for other reasons. If you have been very diligent and have made substantial sacrifices to become completely debt-free, and then have finished saving up a minimum of three months living expenses for emergency use only, I suggest a substantial reward.

If you're like me, you may choose a tropical vacation. Las Brisas is a beautiful resort overlooking Acapulco Bay. Each casita has its own private yard and private swimming pool. The Phoenician, in Scottsdale, Arizona, is an incredible resort. Their *Center for Well Being* offers a very luxurious, relaxing experience. Find something that motivates you and set a goal to enjoy that experience.

I bring these things up because the purpose of this course is not to persuade you to live like a miser, or to deprive you of any enjoyment in life. I strongly believe in enjoying your life and your relationships. Life's too short to postpone happiness.

After getting completely out of debt and building up your emergency fund, you can take your *accelerator* for two or three months and save up for the vacation of a lifetime. Then come home relaxed and rejuvenated, with a new spark in your marriage, and start accumulating wealth for your retirement.

NOTES:

Pay Yourself *Last*

Yes, this is a cheap attempt to get your attention by contradicting what everyone has always heard, "Pay yourself first." The fact is, if you can come up with the self-discipline to pay yourself first (that is, to save 10% of your income off the top then live on the rest), you should be able to come up with the self-discipline to implement this even more effective strategy.

Financial professionals have always recommended saving 10% of your income to invest for your future. This is good advice, but I think it could be better. Professionals generally accept a house payment and a "reasonable" amount of consumer debt as the norm, and don't even think about how much better you could do if you had no debt at all.

Paying yourself first, on a monthly basis, is actually a great idea. But if you take the time to get completely out of debt first, instead of struggling to save 10% of your income, you should be able to comfortably save 30-50% of your income every month.

The money you will save from not paying interest, and the amount you will be able to build up for retirement will bless your life far beyond what you were probably expecting before you completed this course. And the benefit that the stress-reduction will have on your marriage and other relationships cannot be measured in dollars.

Let's look at an example. If your household income is $60,000 per year, and you are in a position to save 10% of your income for retirement, your retirement account could look like this (tax-deferred retirement fund earning 10% per year, $500 monthly contribution):

Year	Balance	Year	Balance	Year	Balance
1	6,283	11	119,430	21	425,725
2	13,223	12	138,219	22	476,587
3	20,891	13	158,975	23	532,775
4	29,361	14	181,905	24	594,846
5	38,719	15	207,235	25	663,417
6	49,056	16	235,218	26	739,168
7	60,475	17	266,131	27	822,851
8	73,091	18	300,282	28	915,297
9	87,027	19	338,008	29	1,017,424
10	102,422	20	379,684	30	1,130,244

This doesn't look too bad, especially if you have 30 years until retirement. But let's see what would happen if we used the 10% to get out of debt first, then took the amount you were spending on debt, plus the 10% to invest for retirement (assuming total monthly debt service of $2,500 and a 7-year payoff period):

Notes:

Year	Balance	Year	Balance	Year	Balance
1	-0-	11	176,167	21	1,091,428
2	-0-	12	232,311	22	1,243,411
3	-0-	13	294,334	23	1,411,309
4	-0-	14	362,851	24	1,596,788
5	-0-	15	438,543	25	1,801,690
6	-0-	16	522,161	26	2,028,047
7	-0-	17	614,535	27	2,278,107
8	37,697	18	716,581	28	2,554,351
9	79,341	19	829,314	29	2,859,521
10	125,345	20	953,850	30	3,196,647

Your circumstances will be different that this, but the results should still show this type of improvement. The fact is, receiving interest pays. Paying interest does not. Get out of debt as quickly as possible and operate on a cash basis. Even if you take some of the money to have fun with, you can still end up with a much better lifestyle at retirement.

If you are not in a position to save 10% of your income, don't feel all alone. The national average is less than a 3% savings rate, which is deplorable. This is largely due to the fact that Americans have too much debt because we want everything right now.

The object of this system is to get you to the point where you can save on a regular basis, and even more than 10% of your income. Following this system, unlike the 10% off the top idea, will cause the amount you can save to gradually increase over time. Even if you can't afford to start with 10% of your income, you can get there quickly.

OTHER SAVINGS GOALS

I do suggest saving your percentage each month before living on the rest. But let's not forget your other savings goals. We don't really plan on not buying anything until we retire, do we? Of course not. So how do we deal with buying things that we use to go into debt for?

Simple. It depends how quickly we need them. If it's something that doesn't need to be purchased immediately, I prefer the separate savings account method. In addition to your monthly retirement account contribution, have a separate account to save up for things that you would have gone into debt for before you completed this course.

A pool, room addition, vacation, car, etc., can all be purchased from this account. That way you won't be stealing from your retirement fund all the time. If your need is more substantial, or more urgent, you can resort to liquidating some of your investments, hopefully from a non-qualified account so there are no early-withdrawal penalties.

For example, let's say you need a bigger house. It will cost $50,000 more than you will get for your present home; and you intend to pay cash. First, make sure that this will not prevent you from having enough money to retire comfortably, then see which non-qualified account would be best to pull it out of.

If you intend to use your retirement account for purposes other than retirement, make sure that you don't have all your money in tax-qualified plans. You don't want to incur early withdrawal penalties. Also, before you take money out of the account, always make sure that you can afford to. You will need a substantial amount of money in your retirement account if you want to be comfortable and not take risks with your retirement money. Know how much you will need, and make sure you will have at least that much.

I actually prefer the idea of having separate accounts for retirement and your other savings goals. For example, once all your debts are paid, you could probably save 30% of your income for retirement, and another 10-15% for other goals such as a larger home or addition, vacations, cars, etc. This way you will be in the habit of leaving your retirement nest-egg alone.

After you have been living debt-free and saving the difference for a substantial period of time, you will notice that not only were you able to save a lot more for your retirement, but you actually lived in the present more comfortably, too. By making interest work for you instead of working for it, you can afford your chosen lifestyle more easily, and retire more comfortably when that time comes.

Write out one long-term and one short-term financial goal:

~ Your Retirement Goal ~

The whole purpose of this workbook is to help you to accumulate plenty of money to retire on so that you can have a happy, healthy, low-stress lifestyle. Simply put, I want to help you to be able to enjoy the rest of your life without ever having to worry about money.

In order to do that, it is important to know how much money you will need to retire on, so you can set your goal to accumulate at least that amount of money. If you would now need $2,500/month, for example – if you were debt free, of course – to live your idea of a comfortable life, we have to know three things:

1. How much will $2,500 in today's dollars be when you retire?

2. How much will you have to accumulate to produce that amount every month for the rest of your life?

3. What will it take to accumulate that amount of money before you retire?

These are very important questions. First of all, due to inflation, the monthly amount you would need to live comfortably right now is going to be higher when you retire. If you need $2,500 per month right now, but you're not going to retire for 30 years, assuming 4% inflation per year, you would actually need over $8,000/month when you retire! If you set your goal to have $2,500/month at retirement, and you reach that goal, you'll be very disappointed when you discover that it takes over $8,000 to do the same thing that $2,500 does today.

Second, you have to know how much you need to accumulate in your retirement savings in order to produce that amount of income for you each month. And you have to take into consideration that when you're retired, you're not earning more money to invest so you have to be careful not to take too much risk. If you lose part of your retirement savings, the amount you have left will produce a lower monthly income.

Third, you have to have some kind of a plan to accumulate the amount of savings you'll need to produce the monthly income you want. But it's hard to do that if you have no idea of how much you want to have in savings.

Let's address each of these three steps in order:

(1)   <u>How much income will you need to retire on each month?</u>

That depends on you. Using the information and worksheets in this workbook, you should be able to add up how much it would take you to live comfortably if all your debts are paid off. Since the goal is to have all your debts paid off, that amount is acceptable – as long as you're going to stick with this plan.

You can reduce this monthly amount by any known benefits you will definitely receive during your retirement. Government benefits, pensions, etc. can take care of part of this monthly amount. I prefer to not consider these things, but you can if you need to or want to. Just make sure to not deduct those amounts from your monthly needs amount until you've increased your monthly amount for inflation.

To continue, let's use an example. Let's say that the amount you have decided you will need to live on at retirement, considering any expected changes in lifestyle or expenditures (increased healthcare costs, travel, etc.) is $2,500 per month.

The next thing we have to do is to figure out how much that $2,500 per month translates to in terms of future dollars. How much will $2,500 per month in today's dollars really be when you retire? Let's say that you want to retire in 20 years. You can use a financial calculator to figure this out; but let's keep it simple & use the Rule of 72 that we went over earlier.

You can guess at whatever rate of inflation you want to use for your calculation, since no one really knows exactly how much it will be. I'd suggest assuming 4-

5%, since that seems to fall into the average range over time. Using a higher rate of inflation will give you a better buffer zone for your predictions, but it will make it more difficult to achieve the goal because it will require a higher account balance to be accumulated.

Using the Rule of 72, if we assume 4% inflation:

$$72 \div 4 = 18$$

That means that if we assume a 4% rate of inflation, the $2,500 per month that you would need now will actually double to $5,000 per month needed in 18 years. If you want to retire in 20 years, you will need some amount in excess of $5,000 per month.

Instead of getting too technical with the math calculations, let's just assume that you will need $5,500 per month to retire on if you are to retire in 20 years. That's actually very close to what my financial calculator told me would be the exact amount needed at that time.

(2)   How much will you have to save up over the next 20 years in order to create an income of $5,500 per month?

There are actually two different ways to calculate this, and you can choose which you prefer. Again, one of them allows a little better buffer zone for unanticipated changes, but that one is harder to achieve because it will require a higher retirement savings balance.

A. The first method is to figure out how much you would have to accumulate in order for that account balance to produce a monthly interest amount of $5,500. You would be able to live off the interest only so your principal balance would not go down while you're spending your interest. In this case, you should have a nice account balance to leave to your heirs when you leave this planet.

Calculating this amount is very simple. First, we have to take a guess at what rate of return we will receive on our retirement account, considering an acceptable level of risk. I do not recommend accepting a high degree of risk with your retirement account because if you lose your money, you will not be able to recover that loss by working and saving it up again.

For purposes of this example, let's assume that we can get a 6% annual return while our money is safe enough to meet our comfort level. There is a simple formula we can use to determine how much we need to save up to produce $5,500/month at 6% interest:

Since 6% is our annual return, 6 ÷ 12 months, or 0.5%, would be our monthly return. Because we're dealing with a monthly income goal instead of stating it as an annual goal, let's use 0.5% instead of 6%. Here's our formula:

$$\$5,500 \div 0.5\% = \$1,100,000$$

According to this simple formula, we will need $1,100,000 saved up in our retirement account(s), producing 0.5% per month (6% per year) in order to have a monthly income of $5,500. If it is easier, you can multiply the $5,500 by 12 months and use 6% like this:

$$\$5,500 \times 12 \text{ months} = \$66,000/\text{year}$$

$$\$66,000 \div 0.06 = \$1,100,000$$

Either method will give you the same answer. Use the one you're more comfortable with. This is the first and more difficult way to determine how much we will need to save to meet our monthly income requirement at retirement.

B. The second, or easier way to meet this goal is not actually easier to calculate; but it is easier to save up for. This method allows you to use some of your principal to live off of during retirement so you don't have to save up as much money in order to retire. With this method, you would plan to use up most of your retirement savings and not leave it to your heirs.

With this method, you have to estimate how long you're going to live. Yeah, that sounds fun, doesn't it? We need that estimate because we're going to figure out how much money you will need to live for the rest of your life if your savings is to be exhausted at the end of that period. This requires a lower account balance because part of your monthly income is going to be from your principal balance.

That is a little more complicated to calculate, and if you intend to use this method, I do suggest that you consult a financial professional. You don't want to make a mistake with this and run out of money while you're still alive. I would suggest assuming a little extra time if you choose this option.

If we assume that the person in the example above will live for 20 years of retirement, here's how I would use my financial calculator to answer this question:

n (number of compounding periods) = **240** (20 years x 12 months per year)

i (interest rate) = **0.5** (6% ÷ 12 months)

PV (present value) = (leave blank for now – this is what we're solving for)

PMT (monthly payment) = **$5,500**. This is our desired monthly income.

FV (future value) = **0** (zero) because we are planning on using up the entire principal balance over the 20-year retirement period.

Now, we go back and press **PV** and get the answer **-767,694**. We would need to have $767,694 in our retirement account in order to be able to pull out $5,500 per month for 20 years, assuming a fixed return of 0.5% per month. The answer is expressed as a negative number because we entered our monthly amount as a positive number. Don't worry about why that is; it would just complicate things to explain it here.

For simplicity, let's call this number $768,000. This is significantly less than the $1,100,000 we would have to save up if we do not want to live on principal as well as interest. The method you choose will probably be influenced by how realistic you consider it to save up one of these amounts.

For example, you may go through all the steps in this workbook and determine that it is realistic for you to save $800,000 before retirement but not $1,100,000. If that is the case, you may decide that the second method is right for you. Or you may determine that it is realistic for you to save up $1,100,000. If so, you may be comfortable living on interest only without having to tap into your principal balance. It is really up to you. I just want you to know about both options.

(3)   How do I accumulate that amount before I retire?

After going through the steps in this workbook, you should have some sort of estimate as to how much you will be able to invest for your retirement and for how long. If you use a financial calculator, it will be very easy to calculate how much you can accumulate at a given rate of return. If you don't use a financial calculator, use the Rule of 72 to get an estimate.

For example, let's say that you decided you want to save up $1,100,000 for retirement, and you will have 18 years to save after getting rid of all your debt. You are comfortable being aggressive and are assuming a 12% rate of return during the time you are saving, then you will move into more conservative investments when it's time for you to retire.

$$72 \div 12 = 6$$

That means your money will double every 6 years. If you have 18 years to save, your money will double three times. Since you're saving something every month, it won't be as easy as taking the $1,100,000 number and dividing it in half three times – that would only work if you were going to place a large sum of money into an account right now and not add to it for 18 years.

The easiest way to do that would be to start with your estimate of how much you will be able to invest every year and double it the number of times that money will be in the account. I don't want to spend too much time on this, because it's not going to be the most accurate way to calculate this. But it is something you can play with to get an idea of how your money will multiply at different rates of return.

I really think the best way to do this is with a financial calculator or an online financial program. If you hate numbers, find someone who can run the calculation for you. Here's how I would do this with my financial calculator:

The goal is $1,100,000 and I have 18 years to save up. Let's use a little more realistic interest rate of 10% per year. That's still aggressive but a little less risky than trying to get 12%. Here are my calculator entries:

n = 216 (18 years x 12 months)

i = 0.8333 (10% ÷ 12 months)

PV = 0 (I'm going to pay in monthly, not starting with any lump sum.)

PMT = leave blank; this is what we're solving for.

FV = 1,100,000 (this is the amount we want to have after 18 years.

Next, we press the **PMT** key and get our answer of **$-1,831.61**/month. This is a negative number because it is an outflow, not an inflow. This is the amount we'll have to save each month for 18 years, assuming a 10% fixed return, in order to accumulate our $1,100,000.

If I am Mr. or Mrs. Jones, that is great news because I can actually save as much as $2,850/month once my debts are gone. In that case, I may do the calculation again, assuming a lower rate of return so I can get away with accepting a lower degree of risk. I may also set my goal a bit higher so I can enjoy an even better lifestyle in my retirement years. By planning ahead and learning how to work this system, I can trade in my debt for a prosperous, wealthy retirement.

Now, try working on your own example:

(1)   How much will I need or want to retire on each month in 'future dollars'?

(2)   How much do I need to accumulate in my retirement account in order to produce the monthly amount I want?

(3)   How much will I have to put aside each month for retirement, over the period of time I will have, to accomplish that savings goal?

Notes:

MISC.

CARS

By now, you've probably gotten the impression that I don't think it's a great idea to go into debt for consumer items – I certainly hope so. However, in the real world, sometimes it is necessary to use debt temporarily to pay for an automobile. For many people, there just isn't a realistic option to do without a reliable vehicle until you have accumulated enough savings to pay cash for it. If you want to earn money, you have to be able to get to your job and back so you can do the work you're paid to do.

In addition to having to be able to get to work and function in life, for some types of work a certain type of late model vehicle is actually required in order to get or succeed at the job. For example, if you're a real estate agent specializing in upper-end homes in the Scottsdale, Arizona area, you can't function properly driving around in a rusted out, dinged up, fifteen year old car with no air conditioning. If you want your clients to take you seriously, you need to look successful – I understand that.

So, whether it's basic, reliable transportation you need or something a bit fancier, if you have to go into debt to purchase an automobile, what is the best way to do it?

The mistake most people make is that they will go down to a new car dealership that offers low-priced new cars, and drive home in something shiny and new so they can feel that rush of excitement that only the new car smell can provide – while justifying their decision to pay for this new car, over the maximum time period available, of course, with the fact that they have a new car warranty so they do have the reliable transportation they need.

The problem is that this kind of car purchase puts a person in an "upside down" position that is hard to get out from under – even over time. Typically, this is what happens:

1. You don't have much cash, but you know you need reliable transportation.
2. Because you won't be able to qualify for or pay for a large monthly payment and high maintenance costs, such as when buying an expensive vehicle from one of the finer import dealers, you go down to the new car dealership that offers the lowest-priced cars available. This place has TV commercials non-stop that show you how inexpensive it is to drive one of their shiny new cars, and they're getting inside your head.
3. You become convinced that this is the right choice because the monthly payment is manageable and a new car has a new car warranty, and thus, your risk of having to pay for unexpected repairs is very small and you now have reliable transportation. In addition, it just plain feels good to drive a brand new car.
4. This type of car depreciates very rapidly, and may not remain in good condition as long as a more expensive car would; so you start thinking about trading it in about halfway into the financing period.

5. You find out that you still owe much more on the car than its trade-in value, but the new car dealer shows you how they can roll that negative equity into the new loan and still give you another new car for a monthly payment you think you can afford.

6. Now, you're driving another new car that will also depreciate quickly though the amount you owe on it will go down more slowly – and you have the added disadvantage of having borrowed too much against the vehicle to begin with, because you rolled in the negative equity from your previous car. So, good luck ever getting out from under that upside down situation and having a vehicle paid for while it's still worth driving.

This scenario happens so often that many car dealers get rich (or richer) from exactly what I just described above. Allow me to explain how this happens and what to do to make sure it doesn't happen to you.

There are actually two negative things working at the same time in this scenario, that almost guarantee that you will remain "upside down" unless you keep the car for much longer than you would like to.

The first one is that when you buy any new car, but especially one of the less-expensive models that isn't very good at holding its value, you're going to suffer a big loss the moment you drive the car off the lot. From there, it will continue to go down in value faster than your monthly payments can reduce the principal balance owed, which brings us to the second negative.

When you are in the beginning phase of paying off any fully-amortized loan (a loan with principal and interest in each payment that pays off the balance over the loan term), a very large part of each monthly payment is going towards interest, not principal. That means that a relatively small part of each payment is reducing the amount of the debt you owe.

What this means to you is that both of these things are happening at the same time:

1. Each monthly payment you make does very little to reduce your balance;
2. The vehicle you're paying on loses a large percentage of its value.

This creates a situation where you will be so upside down on the vehicle, that you are not likely to be able to recover from this until long after you think you are ready to trade in that car for a new one.

I would like to illustrate exactly what I'm talking about here. Different cars have different depreciation rates, of course; but let's just use as a general example a new car that depreciates 30% in the first year and 20% every year after that. This won't be exactly what happens to you, but it will certainly be close enough to illustrate my point with reasonable accuracy. (Remember that we're talking about dealer trade-in value here, so this is probably pretty accurate for the type of car I'm talking about.)

At the same time, let's say that you take out a loan for the full price of the car, paying as a down payment only the tax, title and license. Your term is 6 years and your interest rate is 9%. Again, this will probably not be your exact experience –

some will be better, and some worse. Many times these car dealers will finance the full price of the car, plus the tax, title and license, plus the amount you were upside down in the vehicle you're trading in. On top of that, interest rates can be a lot higher than what we're using in the example, so this example is not unrealistic.

In this example, here is what the car will be worth at the end of each year for 6 years, the term of the loan:

Year 0	$20,000 (purchase price)
Year 1	$14,000
Year 2	$11,200
Year 3	$8,960
Year 4	$7,168
Year 5	$5,734.40
Year 6	$4,587.52

This may seem dramatic, but I have seen cars depreciate more rapidly than this. Some of these cars are actually practically worthless after six years. So, let's say that this is close enough for our example.

Now, let's take a look at how much you still owe on the car at the end of each of these six years:

(next page…)

Year 0 $20,000 (full loan balance at time of purchase)

Year 1 $17,367.02

Year 2 $14,487.05

Year 3 $11,336.91

Year 4 $7,891.27

Year 5 $4,122.41

Year 6 $0 (loan paid in full)

You can guess what we're going to do now, right? We're going to compare the two sets of numbers and look at how much positive or negative equity you have in the car at the end of each of the six years:

Year	Equity
0	0 (date of purchase)
1	-$3,367.02
2	-$3,287.05
3	-$2,376.91
4	-$723.27
5	$1,611.99
6	$4,587.52 (date car is paid off)

Let's look at a picture of these curves so we can see what we're talking about here:

(next page...)

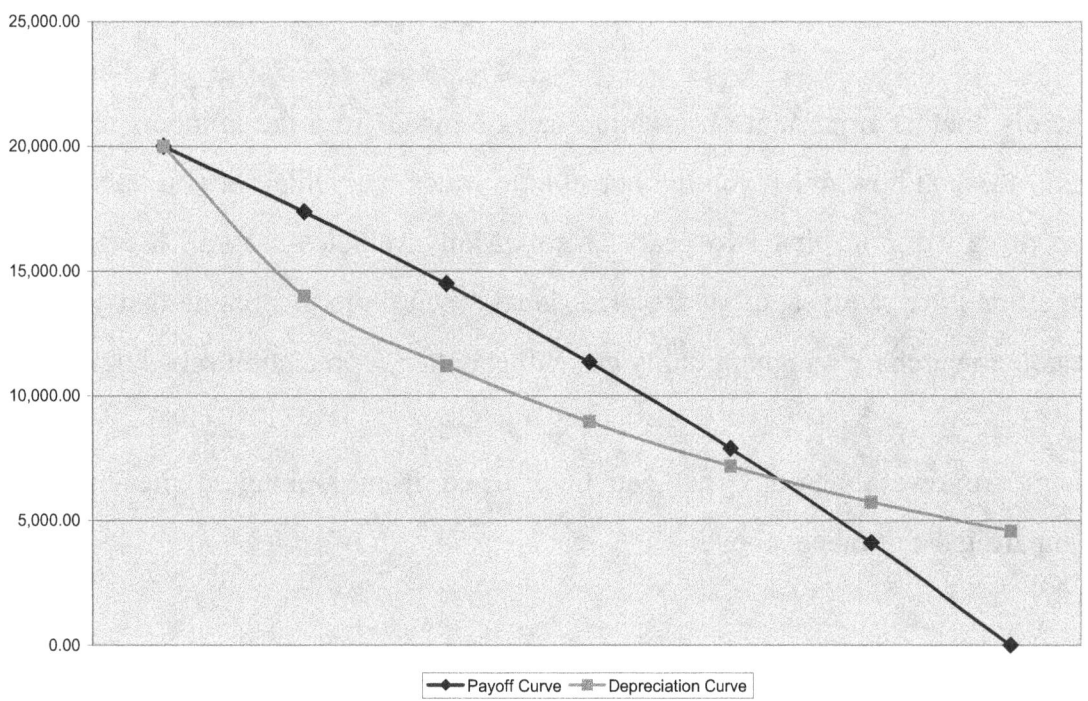

Payoff vs. Depreciation

Payoff Curve — Depreciation Curve

The entire time that the Depreciation Curve is underneath the Payoff Curve, you are upside down in the vehicle – you owe more than it's worth. In the real world, this looks fairly modest to me. I have – in the past, thankfully – been $8,000 to $10,000 upside down in vehicles in this general price range, and it is very common for people to be $4,000 to $6,000 or more upside down at the time they start shopping for a new car.

The most important thing to notice is not how much you are upside down at any given point, though that is important. The most important thing to notice is how long you have to pay on this car before you are no longer upside down. In our example, it takes over four years before you even start accumulating any equity in the vehicle at all. I believe that most people begin thinking about a new car after two to three years.

There's another important observation can be made from the numbers above, as well. Look at how much you may be able to save on a vehicle if you let someone else drive it for its first two years or so. Many vehicles are still in very good condition after two years, but the price is so much more affordable that you may be able to purchase a higher quality car with a better depreciation schedule.

There are several lessons that can be learned from looking at the chart and comparing the numbers above:

1. Try to find a car that is two to three years old instead of purchasing a new one. That way, someone else has suffered the dramatic loss in value that occurs in the first two years – not you.

2. Never finance a car for a longer period of time than you realistically expect to keep it. Think carefully about this when you go to purchase a car. You know how beautiful it is new, but are you really going to want to keep this car when it's four or five years old?

3. Whether you intended to or not, try to keep your car until it is paid off. It is very expensive to trade in automobiles frequently, especially if you buy new ones; and it takes time to get in a positive equity position in a rapidly-depreciating vehicle. The least you can do for yourself for making all those payments is to make sure you have some equity in your vehicle when you go to trade it in.

4. Finance your car for the shortest period that you can afford to. If you must finance your automobile purchase, look at the three or four year option instead of going straight for the six year option. If you can't afford the payments for a shorter term, consider your options at a lower price point before agreeing to pay for the car for six years. Remember that many people do not want to keep their car for six years, especially the type of car that most people can afford to buy new.

5. When you are in a position to pay cash for your vehicles, it is still best to let someone else enjoy the first two years in the vehicle – and pay for that privilege, of course. If you buy cars that are two years old and hold them for four years, you're doing pretty well. Remember that even if you're paying cash, it is expensive to trade your cars in too often.

Another thing I should mention is that you can usually purchase a good, comprehensive warranty for a used car – you don't have to buy a new car to get a warranty. If you buy a two-year-old car that is still within the manufacturers warranty period, you should be able to buy a bumper-to-bumper extended warranty for the car.

And if you have been waiting until your cars are paid off before you trade them in, hopefully, you will have enough trade-in value to at least pay for the tax, title, license, and the extended warranty – so that you're only financing the value of the car itself at the time of purchase.

If you purchase your cars after the initial two years of depreciation has already been taken, and then only finance the actual value of the car – and only for the length of time you are really going to keep it – hopefully, you'll wind up with enough equity in the old car to cover the tax, title, license, and warranty on your next car so that you'll only have to finance that car's actual value as well.

Then, if you've also saved up a down payment for your newer car, you should be able to shorten the financing term, which will mean that you'll have more residual value in the vehicle at the time it's paid off. That with the opportunity to continue driving the car with no payments will mean that you can save up more of a down payment before trading in the newer car.

If you create a positive spiral like this, instead of the negative spiral of trading in your vehicles while in a negative equity position and rolling that negative equity into the new loan, you should eventually be able to start paying cash for your cars instead of financing them. When you drive a car that is paid for instead of one you're making payments on, you can save money every month for your next car instead of paying on the one you're already driving.

When you can save to pay cash for your next car instead of making payments on the one you're already driving, you're collecting interest instead of paying it. That means more money for you and less for the creditors. You have just become one of the people who collect interest instead of one of the people who pay interest. Congratulations, you've graduated.

Another point I'd like to make for those of you who, like me, really enjoy buying brand-new cars and might tend to resist doing the more sensible thing and buying them gently used is this:

No one drives a new car – everybody drives a used car – if it's being driven, it's used! Unless it's only a test drive and the dealer still owns it, if you're driving a car, it's used. Remember that even if you buy the car brand-new, once you buy it and leave the dealership in it, it's used. So, you're going to drive a used car anyway – the only difference is who's been using it. You'll save a lot of money if you let the car be used by someone else for the first two years – but either way, you're going to drive a used car.

Once you've used this book to accumulate a good amount of wealth, buying a brand-new car may be an indulgence you decide to allow yourself – and I may be right there with you. But while you're still in the stage of getting out of debt and accumulating enough money so that your money can work for you instead of you working for your money, remember that it can really help you to get ahead if you're sensible instead of emotional about your automobile purchases.

_____

What are you going to do differently next time you purchase an automobile?

_____

If You Cannot Presently Pay All Your Bills

If you do not feel that you can implement the techniques in this book because you can't even pay all your bills right now, this section is for you. If this is not your situation, it is probably not important that you read this section.

I mentioned early in the book during the Jones example that even if you do not have an extra $100 (or any extra amount) to accelerate your payoff, the system will still work, and you can be out of debt much more quickly than you probably think you can.

But what if you can't even keep up with your minimum payments right now? In this section, we will discuss some possible options that you may have. The important thing to keep in mind is this:

> **You MUST put yourself in a position to be able to take advantage of the techniques presented in this book, or you will probably have financial difficulties for the rest of your life.**

The good news is that there probably is a way to accomplish this. We need to go through the options and see which are right for you.

Let's assume that right now, you are unable to pay all the minimum payments due on all of your debts. There are more people in this position than you probably realize. There are several options that you should consider. After going through all the options, you should decide which of them will work for you, then TAKE ACTION! Do not think that ignoring the problem will make it go away. That usually only makes it worse.

First, find out where all your money is going. This may be easier said than done. But it's important. You must know, as closely as possible, where all your money goes, so that you can determine what changes you might be able to make to improve your situation. The budget sheet included in this workbook can help you to figure this out.

Look at your expenses. Where can you cut back? If you look carefully, you will see that those small expenses really do add up. Can you take your lunch to work, eat at home more often, quit smoking, quit spending so much money on unnecessary items, etc.?

How much of a monthly shortfall do you have? If it is a small amount, can you work extra, just long enough to pay off one bill, so your "monthly nut" will be manageable? Do you own something that you could sell, that would bring in enough money to put you in a break-even position every month?

After you have gone through your finances, if you have determined that you cannot do anything that would make enough difference to make you break even every month, don't give up. We're not done yet. And you must find a way to at least break even every month. If you are not getting ahead, you are falling behind. And I know you don't want to keep falling behind; otherwise you wouldn't have bought this book.

You must realize that if you get too far behind, you will either be bankrupt, or you will start having things repossessed. Even drastic action on your part, can be preferable to those circumstances. So think of some ideas like the following, that relate to your specific situation.

Do you have an expensive car payment? It might be better to give the car back to the bank, and buy a cheap car with what you owe in back payments, rather than continuing to fall further and further behind. (This one hurts, I know.)

Is there any other item that you could give back to a creditor, instead of continuing to pay for? I know this idea is uncomfortable, but it's a lot better than continuing to fall behind every month until you lose everything.

Once you can get yourself into a break-even position, then you can start on the program outlined in this book, and buy practically anything you want, in good time. It's much better to sacrifice some specific item(s) now, than it is to continue a financial course that will get you nowhere.

Don't File Bankruptcy Yet

In no way is this section (or any section of this book) intended to be legal advice, or specific advice for any given person or situation. There are, however, some tactics that have worked for others; and I thought you might like to know about them.

Here's a great idea. Separate your debts into two categories, secured and unsecured. Secured debts are those where the creditor can repossess the item you borrowed the money for, if you don't pay the bill. Unsecured debt, does not allow the creditor to attach the debt to any specific item of your property, so they cannot repossess anything. (They can, in many states, get a judgement against you and may be able to garnish your wages, etc.)

With the secured debts, figure out which items you might be willing to give back in order to reduce your monthly 'nut'. With the unsecured debts, there is often much more you can do to reduce your monthly outflow. Here are several ideas:

1) Let's say you have ten unsecured creditors. (This is not uncommon.) Your monthly payments on these accounts total $1,000. (This is also not uncommon.) Here's what you do:

Call each one of the creditors, and nicely explain that your debt situation has gotten way out of control, and you are *"trying to avoid bankruptcy"*. The only way you can do this is to offer a reduced monthly payment to each creditor, say $25. You are willing to do this, *only* if they will immediately stop all interest charges, late fees, and over the limit fees.

You may settle for more than $25 for some creditors, just get it as low as you can. The important thing is to (1) reduce your monthly outflow, and (2) stop all additional charges. Tell them that this is the best you can do, and it is certainly more money than they will get from you if you file bankruptcy.

This tactic can be of great benefit to you, as from now on, every dime you pay to these creditors will reduce the principal balance you owe them. Not only have you cut your payments in half or less, but you have also completely eliminated all those other charges that keep you in debt for what seems like forever.

It is important that you figure out in advance exactly how much you will be able to pay monthly, before you commit yourself to it. Once you start this type of arrangement with your creditors, you need to keep up with it.

If you are consistently reliable with your payment, the creditor may even be willing to open your account again when you can resume normal payments. You will probably be better off continuing as you are, with your account closed, making interest-free, reduced payments until your account is paid in full.

It may be that some of your creditors will not be anxious to accommodate your request for a reduced, interest and penalty-free payment plan unless you motivate them. Basically, this means you don't make the payments for a few months, so they feel lucky you're offering to pay them anything.

One tactic is to withhold payment from all unsecured creditors for two months, and use the money you saved to completely pay off one or two of them. Then you apply the idea above to the rest of them. Now you have one or two fewer debts to deal with, which will help your cash flow.

Another idea is to settle with your creditors for a reduced cash amount, to have your account "paid in full". Once again, your creditors will probably not be receptive to this idea if they are receiving reliable and complete monthly payments. If you haven't paid them in several months, however, and you call them up and say, "My dad said he'd give me the money to pay you guys off, if you'll take 50 cents on the dollar. That's the only way I'll have of paying you anything for at least five years", they may take what they can get and be done with it.

If you do this, make sure you can pay what you agree to. Maybe a relative will loan you the money for this type of arrangement. You might be able to scrape together enough to do this one at a time, just by what you save every month using the other ideas above. Whatever. Just make sure that you have the agreement in writing before you pay them, so they don't take your money and keep billing you for more. You want the account marked *Paid In Full.*

Once you have applied the above ideas and you now are in a break-even situation, don't stop there. Now you can go back through this book and start on a program to get ahead financially – and fast. Whatever you do, don't take on more debt you can't afford. Old habits die hard, but kill them!

No one will do this for you. *You* must do it. And you will probably never get ahead if you don't force yourself to develop the right financial habits. Read this book as many times as it takes for it to really sink in. You should *want* to do the things discussed in this book, because they will help you to have a better life. And that's what we all want, isn't it?

Okay. What if you've gone through all the ideas listed above and then some, and you still can't put yourself in a "break-even" situation to start this *Trading Debt for Wealth* program? Well, you may have to consider bankruptcy. It's not the end of the world. It's certainly not as bad as never being in a position that will allow you to get ahead. Check with your attorney, and get the details.

The point is this: Whatever it takes, you must put yourself in at least a break-even situation so you can start this program, or you will probably always have financial troubles. And that's no way to live.

(Note -- The ideas in this section are not offered as a way to rip-off creditors. These techniques should be used only when necessary, as an alternative to bankruptcy. They are, in fact, better for your creditors than a bankruptcy is.)

List 3 things <u>you</u> can do to get current and start "Trading Debt for Wealth":

(1)

(2)

(3)

Notes:

IN CONCLUSION

The purpose of this workbook was to accomplish three things:

1) To help you see the huge impact that paying interest can have on your long-term financial situation, and to convince you that it is worth the trouble and patience required to start receiving – instead of paying – compound interest.

2) To help you come up with a plan of attack that will have all your debts paid off, in a fraction of the time you thought it would take.

3) To help you understand what to do with all that money you were spending on servicing your debt; so that you can maximize your profits, minimize your taxes, and end up having hundreds of thousands, or even millions of dollars more than you expected to when you retire.

If this book helps your life to be better than it would have been, by putting more money in your pocket for your retirement and other goals, then I have accomplished my goal.

There are many investment opportunities, products and strategies that have not been discussed in this workbook. I would encourage further study into your areas of interest. Numerous books, magazines, and professionals are waiting for you.

What are the 3 most important things that you learned from this workbook?

(1)

(2)

(3)